Unlocking Happiness
A Holistic Approach to Healing Mental Health Disorders

Ryan Parekh

Unlocking Happiness A Holistic Approach to Healing Mental Health Disorders

Copyright © 2023 by Ryan Parekh

The first edition was published in 2023

ISBN:
Published by:
Sunshine
1663 Liberty Drive
Hyderabad, IN 47403
www.Sunshinepublishers.com

This book is self-published using on-demand printing and publishing, which allows it to be printed and distributed globally.

TABLE OF CONTENTS

Chapter 1: Understanding Mental Health Disorders

Defining Mental Health

In our fast-paced and often stressful world, mental health has become an increasingly important topic. But what exactly is mental health? Is it simply the absence of mental illness, or does it encompass something more? In this subchapter, we will delve into the various dimensions of mental health, providing you with a comprehensive understanding of this crucial aspect of overall well-being.

Mental health can be defined as a state of emotional, psychological, and social well-being in which an individual is able to cope with the normal stresses of life, work productively, and contribute to their community. It is not merely the absence of mental disorders, but rather a holistic state of balance and harmony within oneself and the surrounding environment.

Understanding the intricacies of mental health is essential to tackle the rising tide of lifestyle diseases that are plaguing our society. Stress, anxiety, depression, and burnout have become alarmingly common, leading to a host of physical ailments such as cardiovascular diseases, obesity, and diabetes. By addressing mental health issues, we can effectively prevent and manage these lifestyle diseases, improving the overall quality of life.

When it comes to mental health, it is important to recognize that it is a continuum. Just as physical health exists on a spectrum, so does mental health. It is not a binary state of being either mentally ill or mentally healthy; rather, individuals can experience varying degrees of mental well-being throughout their lives.

Furthermore, mental health is influenced by various factors. Biological factors such as genetics and brain chemistry play a role, as do life experiences and family history of mental health problems. Additionally, socio-economic factors, such as income level, access to healthcare, and social support, can significantly impact mental health.

To truly unlock happiness and promote mental health, it is crucial to adopt a holistic approach. This involves addressing mental health not only through therapy and medication but also through lifestyle changes. Incorporating practices such as mindfulness, exercise, proper nutrition, and social connection can have a profound impact on mental well-being.

In conclusion, mental health is a multidimensional concept that goes beyond the absence of mental illness. It encompasses emotional, psychological, and social well-being and plays a significant role in preventing and managing lifestyle diseases. By understanding the various factors influencing mental health and adopting a holistic approach, we can unlock happiness and achieve optimal mental well-being.

The Prevalence of Mental Health Disorders

In today's fast-paced world, mental health disorders have become increasingly prevalent. They have emerged as a significant concern, affecting people from all walks of life. From anxiety and depression to more severe conditions like bipolar disorder and schizophrenia, these disorders can have a profound impact on an individual's overall well-being. Understanding the prevalence of mental health disorders is crucial for anyone concerned about their mental health or the well-being of their loved ones.

Research indicates that mental health disorders are incredibly common, with millions of people worldwide experiencing them at some point in their lives. In fact, the World Health Organization estimates that approximately one in four individuals will be affected by mental health disorders at some point in their lives. These disorders do not discriminate based on age, gender, or socioeconomic status. They can affect anyone, regardless of their background or lifestyle.

The prevalence of mental health disorders has been linked to various factors. Lifestyle diseases, such as obesity, diabetes, and heart disease, have been found to have a significant impact on mental health. The stress and emotional toll of these conditions can lead to the development or worsening of mental health disorders. Additionally, unhealthy lifestyle habits, such as poor diet, lack of exercise, and substance abuse, can also contribute to the prevalence of mental health disorders.

It is essential to recognize the signs and symptoms of mental health disorders to seek early intervention and treatment. Some common indicators include persistent feelings of sadness, anxiety, or irritability, changes in sleep patterns, loss of interest in activities once enjoyed, difficulty concentrating, and thoughts of self-harm or suicide. If you or someone you know is experiencing these symptoms, it is crucial to reach out for help and support.

Fortunately, there is hope for those struggling with mental health disorders. With a holistic approach to healing, individuals can unlock happiness and regain control of their lives. This approach encompasses various strategies, including therapy, medication, lifestyle changes, and support from loved ones. By addressing the root causes and implementing a comprehensive treatment plan, individuals can improve their mental health and overall well-being.

In summary, mental health disorders are prevalent in today's society, affecting millions of individuals worldwide. Lifestyle diseases and unhealthy habits can contribute to their prevalence. Recognizing the signs and symptoms and seeking early intervention is crucial for effective treatment. With a holistic approach to healing, individuals can unlock happiness and experience a renewed sense of well-being. Remember, you are not alone, and there is help available.

Common Types of Mental Health Disorders

In today's fast-paced world, mental health disorders have become increasingly prevalent, affecting individuals from all walks of life. These disorders, often referred to as lifestyle diseases, can have a profound impact on one's overall well-being and happiness. Understanding the common types of mental health disorders is crucial in order to address and heal these conditions effectively.

1. Anxiety Disorders: Anxiety disorders encompass a range of conditions, including generalized anxiety disorder, panic disorder, and social anxiety disorder. Those affected by anxiety disorders often experience excessive worry, fear, and feelings of unease, which can significantly disrupt their daily lives.

2. Mood Disorders: Mood disorders, such as depression and bipolar disorder, are characterized by significant changes in mood and emotional states. Depression involves persistent feelings of sadness, hopelessness, and a loss of interest in activities once enjoyed. Bipolar disorder, on the other hand, involves extreme shifts in mood, from manic episodes of high energy and euphoria to depressive episodes.

3. Eating Disorders: Eating disorders, such as anorexia nervosa, bulimia nervosa, and binge eating disorder, are complex conditions that affect an individual's relationship with food and body image. These disorders can have severe physical and psychological consequences if left untreated.

4. Substance Use Disorders: Substance use disorders refer to the misuse or addiction to substances such as alcohol, drugs, or prescription medications. These disorders often have a significant impact on an individual's mental and physical health, as well as their relationships and overall quality of life.

5. Personality Disorders: Personality disorders involve long-standing patterns of behavior, thoughts, and emotions that significantly deviate from societal norms. Examples of personality disorders include borderline personality disorder,

narcissistic personality disorder, and obsessive-compulsive personality disorder.

6. Post-Traumatic Stress Disorder (PTSD): PTSD is a mental health disorder that can develop after experiencing or witnessing a traumatic event. Those with PTSD may experience flashbacks, nightmares, and severe anxiety related to the traumatic event.

7. Attention-Deficit/Hyperactivity Disorder (ADHD): ADHD is a neurodevelopmental disorder that affects both children and adults. It is characterized by persistent patterns of inattention, hyperactivity, and impulsivity, which can significantly impact an individual's daily functioning and relationships.

Understanding the common types of mental health disorders is the first step towards promoting healing and well-being. By recognizing the symptoms and seeking appropriate support and treatment, individuals can regain control over their lives and unlock happiness. Remember, mental health disorders are not a reflection of weakness or personal failure. With compassion, understanding, and the right tools, anyone can embark on a holistic journey towards healing and well-being.

Depression

Depression: Navigating the Shadows

In today's fast-paced and ever-evolving world, mental health disorders have become increasingly pervasive, and depression stands out as one of the most prevalent. In this subchapter, we dive deep into the depths of depression, shedding light on its various facets, its impact on our lives, and the holistic approach to finding healing and unlocking happiness.

Depression is not merely a passing phase of sadness or feeling down; it is a complex and multifaceted mental health disorder that affects millions around the globe. It goes beyond the occasional blues and can manifest as a persistent feeling of emptiness, hopelessness, and a loss of interest or pleasure in activities once enjoyed. It affects not only the mind but also the body, often leading to physical symptoms such as fatigue, changes in appetite, and sleep disturbances.

Understanding depression requires acknowledging its underlying causes. While it can be triggered by external factors such as trauma, loss, or significant life changes, it is important to recognize that depression is not solely a result of personal weakness or character flaws. It is a legitimate medical condition that requires compassion, understanding, and proper treatment.

In this subchapter, we explore various lifestyle diseases and their interconnectedness with depression. We delve into the impact of modern-day stressors, such as work pressure, financial strain, and social isolation, on our mental well-being. We also shed light on how our lifestyle choices, including poor nutrition, lack of exercise, substance abuse, and excessive screen time, can contribute to the development and exacerbation of depression.

Unlocking happiness and healing from depression calls for a holistic approach that addresses the mind, body, and spirit. We delve into evidence-based treatment modalities, including therapy, medication, and alternative approaches, such as mindfulness, meditation, and exercise. By adopting a comprehensive approach, we can empower ourselves to overcome the shadows of depression and embark on a journey towards lasting happiness.

Through personal stories, expert insights, and practical guidance, this subchapter aims to offer a beacon of hope to anyone impacted by depression. Whether you are battling depression yourself or seeking to support a loved one, this chapter equips you with the knowledge and tools to navigate the challenging terrain of depression with empathy, resilience, and a renewed sense of purpose.

Remember, you are not alone in this journey. By unlocking happiness and embracing a holistic approach to mental health, we can break free from the chains of depression and embark on a life filled with joy, meaning, and fulfillment.

Anxiety Disorders

In today's fast-paced world, anxiety disorders have become increasingly prevalent, affecting millions of people globally. This subchapter aims to shed light on the nature of anxiety disorders, their impact on mental health, and provide a holistic approach to healing these conditions. Whether you have personally experienced anxiety or know someone who does, this information is essential for anyone seeking to understand and address this common mental health disorder.

Anxiety disorders encompass a range of conditions, including generalized anxiety disorder (GAD), panic disorder, social anxiety disorder, and specific phobias. These disorders are characterized by excessive worry, fear, and a constant feeling of unease, often interfering with daily life activities. While some level of anxiety is normal, anxiety disorders involve heightened and persistent feelings of distress that can be overwhelming and debilitating.

Unlocking happiness and healing anxiety disorders involves adopting a holistic approach. This means addressing the interconnectedness of our mind, body, and spirit, as these elements play a crucial role in maintaining mental well-being. Understanding the root causes of anxiety is a fundamental step towards healing. Often, anxiety disorders are triggered by a combination of genetic, environmental, and psychological factors. By identifying these triggers and addressing them holistically, individuals can effectively manage and heal their anxiety disorders.

This subchapter will explore various holistic approaches to healing anxiety disorders. It will delve into mindfulness and meditation techniques, which have been proven to reduce anxiety symptoms and promote overall well-being. Additionally, it will discuss the significance of regular exercise and its impact on anxiety management. Engaging in physical activities releases endorphins, which act as natural mood elevators and stress relievers.

Furthermore, this subchapter will explore the importance of a healthy lifestyle in managing anxiety disorders. Proper nutrition, adequate sleep, and stress management techniques are essential components of a well-rounded approach to healing. The book will provide practical tips and strategies for incorporating these lifestyle changes into daily routines.

Ultimately, this subchapter aims to empower readers with a comprehensive understanding of anxiety disorders and equip them with the tools necessary to unlock happiness and healing. By adopting a holistic approach, individuals can take charge of their mental health and embark on a journey towards a brighter, anxiety-free future. Whether you are personally affected by anxiety or seeking to support a loved one, the information provided in this subchapter will serve as a valuable resource in addressing anxiety disorders and promoting overall well-being.

Bipolar Disorder

Bipolar disorder, also known as manic-depressive illness, is a complex mental health condition that affects millions of people worldwide. It is classified as a lifestyle disease due to its impact on an individual's overall well-being and quality of life. In this subchapter, we will delve into the intricacies of bipolar disorder, its symptoms, causes, and available treatment options.

Bipolar disorder is characterized by extreme mood swings that range from manic highs to depressive lows. These episodes can last for days, weeks, or even months, disrupting a person's daily functioning, relationships, and overall stability. During manic episodes, individuals may experience heightened energy levels, euphoria, racing thoughts, and impulsive behavior. On the other hand, depressive episodes are marked by feelings of sadness, hopelessness, fatigue, and lack of interest in previously enjoyed activities.

Understanding the causes of bipolar disorder is crucial in developing an effective treatment plan. While the exact causes remain unknown, research suggests that a combination of genetic, environmental, and neurochemical factors contribute to its development. Family history of bipolar disorder, traumatic life events, substance abuse, and imbalances in brain chemicals such as dopamine and serotonin are known risk factors.

When it comes to managing bipolar disorder, a holistic approach is essential. Treatment typically involves a combination of medication, therapy, and lifestyle adjustments. Medications like mood stabilizers, antipsychotics, and antidepressants are often prescribed to help regulate mood swings and manage symptoms. Psychotherapy, such as cognitive-behavioral therapy (CBT) and interpersonal therapy (IPT), can provide individuals with coping strategies, stress management techniques, and support to navigate their emotions effectively.

In addition to traditional treatments, lifestyle adjustments play a pivotal role in managing bipolar disorder. A balanced diet, regular exercise, and sufficient sleep are crucial components of maintaining stability. Engaging in activities that promote relaxation, such as meditation, yoga, and mindfulness, can also help individuals manage stress and reduce the frequency and severity of episodes.

It is important to remember that bipolar disorder is a chronic condition that requires ongoing management. With the right treatment plan, individuals can lead fulfilling lives and unlock happiness despite their diagnosis. Seeking professional help, building a strong support system, and educating oneself about the disorder are fundamental steps towards healing and living a balanced life.

In conclusion, bipolar disorder is a complex lifestyle disease that affects individuals on various levels, including their emotional, physical, and social well-being. By understanding its symptoms, causes, and available treatment options, individuals can take proactive steps towards managing their condition and finding happiness in their lives. Remember, you are not alone, and there is hope for a brighter future.

Schizophrenia

Schizophrenia: Understanding and Overcoming the Challenges

Schizophrenia is a complex and often misunderstood mental health disorder that affects millions of individuals worldwide. In "Unlocking Happiness: A Holistic Approach to Healing Mental Health Disorders," we delve into the depths of this condition to provide you with a comprehensive understanding of schizophrenia and offer insights on how to manage its challenges.

Chapter 5: Schizophrenia
Subchapter: Understanding and Overcoming the Challenges

Introduction:
In this subchapter, we explore the intricacies of schizophrenia, a mental health disorder that significantly impacts individuals' lives, their families, and society as a whole. We shed light on the various aspects of this condition, including its symptoms, causes, and treatment options. By uncovering the truth behind schizophrenia, we aim to empower individuals, their caregivers, and the wider community to approach this disorder with compassion and knowledge.

1. What is Schizophrenia?
We begin by defining schizophrenia and debunking common misconceptions surrounding it. By explaining the symptoms and the impact it can have on a person's life, we aim to increase awareness and understanding.

2. Causes and Risk Factors:
Next, we delve into the possible causes of schizophrenia, ranging from genetic predisposition to environmental factors. We discuss the importance of recognizing risk factors and early intervention to mitigate the potential impact of the disorder.

3. Diagnosis and Treatment:
We explore the process of diagnosing schizophrenia, highlighting the importance of seeking professional help. We also provide an overview of the available treatment options,

including medication, therapy, and lifestyle changes, emphasizing the benefits of a holistic approach.

4. Living with Schizophrenia: This section offers practical advice and strategies for individuals living with schizophrenia, as well as their loved ones. We discuss ways to manage symptoms, improve quality of life, and foster a supportive environment that promotes recovery and well-being.

5. Breaking the Stigma: Lastly, we address the stigma surrounding schizophrenia and discuss the importance of creating a compassionate and inclusive society. We encourage our readers to challenge stereotypes, increase empathy, and advocate for improved mental health services.

Conclusion:

By understanding the complexities of schizophrenia, we can foster a more supportive and inclusive environment for those affected by this disorder. Through knowledge, empathy, and a holistic approach, we can unlock happiness and help individuals living with schizophrenia thrive.

Note: "Unlocking Happiness: A Holistic Approach to Healing Mental Health Disorders" is a book aimed at anyone seeking to understand and address mental health disorders, including lifestyle diseases. The subchapter on schizophrenia provides a comprehensive overview of the condition and offers practical insights for individuals, caregivers, and the wider community.

Eating Disorders

In today's fast-paced, image-driven society, it's no surprise that many individuals struggle with eating disorders. These disorders, classified under the umbrella term of lifestyle diseases, can have devastating effects on both physical and mental health. In this subchapter, we will explore the various types of eating disorders, their causes, and how a holistic approach can aid in the healing process.

Firstly, it is important to understand that eating disorders come in different forms, the most common being anorexia nervosa, bulimia nervosa, and binge eating disorder. Anorexia nervosa involves an intense fear of gaining weight, leading individuals to restrict their food intake severely. Bulimia nervosa is characterized by episodes of overeating followed by purging through self-induced vomiting or excessive exercise. Binge eating disorder, on the other hand, involves recurrent episodes of uncontrollable eating without any compensatory behaviors.

These disorders can stem from a multitude of factors, including societal pressures, low self-esteem, genetics, and traumatic experiences. It is crucial to address both the underlying causes and the physical symptoms to achieve lasting healing.

A holistic approach to healing eating disorders focuses on treating the whole person – mind, body, and spirit – rather than simply addressing the symptoms. This approach involves various modalities such as therapy, nutrition counseling, mindfulness practices, and self-care techniques.

Therapy, particularly cognitive-behavioral therapy (CBT), can help individuals identify and challenge negative thoughts and behaviors associated with their eating disorder. It provides them with the tools to build a healthier relationship with food and their bodies.

Nutrition counseling plays a vital role in restoring a balanced and nourishing diet. Registered dieticians work closely with individuals to develop personalized meal plans that meet their specific nutritional needs. They also educate about the importance of intuitive eating and mindful food choices.

Mindfulness practices, including meditation and yoga, can aid individuals in developing a healthier body image and self-acceptance. These practices promote self-awareness, reduce stress, and foster a deeper connection between the mind and body.

In addition to these therapeutic techniques, self-care practices such as journaling, engaging in creative outlets, and connecting with a support system can help individuals on their healing journey.

Unlocking happiness and healing from eating disorders requires a comprehensive and compassionate approach. By addressing the root causes, implementing therapeutic techniques, and fostering self-care practices, individuals can begin to rebuild a healthy relationship with food and themselves.

Remember, healing is a journey, and seeking professional help is crucial. With the right support and guidance, anyone can overcome the grasp of an eating disorder and regain their happiness and well-being.

The Impact of Mental Health Disorders on Individuals and Society

Mental health disorders have become a pressing issue in today's society, affecting individuals from all walks of life. In this subchapter, we will explore the profound impact that these disorders have on both individuals and society as a whole. By shedding light on this topic, we hope to increase awareness and understanding surrounding mental health, ultimately paving the way for holistic healing.

When mental health disorders strike, they can significantly disrupt an individual's life. These disorders can manifest in various forms, such as anxiety, depression, bipolar disorder, or schizophrenia. Regardless of the specific disorder, the consequences are often far-reaching. Individuals may experience a decline in their overall well-being, struggling to maintain healthy relationships, perform daily activities, or pursue their goals and passions. The toll on their emotional well-being can be immense, leading to feelings of hopelessness, isolation, and despair.

Moreover, mental health disorders have a ripple effect on society. The burden of these disorders extends beyond the individual, impacting families, communities, and the economy. Families often find themselves grappling with the challenges of supporting and caring for a loved one with a mental health disorder. The strain on relationships, financial resources, and overall quality of life can be overwhelming. As a result, the social fabric of communities may fray, as the needs of individuals with mental health disorders are often misunderstood or stigmatized.

Beyond the personal and familial level, mental health disorders also have a significant economic impact. The cost of mental health care, including medication, therapy, and hospitalization, can be exorbitant, placing a burden on healthcare systems and individuals alike. Additionally, the productivity of individuals with mental health disorders may be compromised, leading to absenteeism, decreased work efficiency, and lost opportunities.

In turn, this affects economic growth and stability on a larger scale.

Addressing the impact of mental health disorders requires a holistic approach that encompasses not only medical interventions but also societal support and understanding. By breaking down stigmas, promoting mental health education, and fostering a compassionate and inclusive society, we can create an environment conducive to healing and well-being.

In conclusion, mental health disorders have a profound impact on both individuals and society. They affect every aspect of a person's life, from their emotional well-being to their ability to function in society. The ripple effect extends to families, communities, and the economy, leaving no one untouched. It is crucial that we recognize the significance of mental health disorders and work together to provide support, understanding, and holistic healing. By doing so, we can unlock happiness and build a healthier, more compassionate society for all.

Chapter 2: The Holistic Approach to Mental Health

What is Holistic Healing?

In today's fast-paced and stressful world, it has become increasingly important to prioritize our mental health. Mental health disorders, often referred to as lifestyle diseases, have become alarmingly common, affecting individuals from all walks of life. However, simply treating the symptoms of these disorders is not enough. To truly heal and achieve happiness, a holistic approach is necessary. This subchapter explores the concept of holistic healing and its significance in addressing mental health disorders.

Holistic healing is a comprehensive approach to healing that takes into account the interconnection between the mind, body, and spirit. It recognizes that mental health disorders cannot be treated in isolation but must be addressed on a deeper level. Rather than focusing solely on managing symptoms, holistic healing aims to identify and address the root causes of these disorders.

At its core, holistic healing emphasizes the importance of treating the whole person rather than just the disease. It recognizes that mental health disorders can stem from various factors, including physical imbalances, emotional trauma, environmental influences, and unhealthy lifestyle choices. By addressing these underlying issues, holistic healing seeks to restore balance and promote overall well-being.

One of the key principles of holistic healing is the belief that the body has an innate ability to heal itself. Holistic practitioners work with individuals to support and enhance this natural healing process. They may utilize a range of therapeutic modalities, including nutrition, exercise, mindfulness practices, energy healing, and counseling. These modalities are chosen based on the individual's unique needs and circumstances, with the aim of restoring harmony and promoting mental, physical, and spiritual wellness.

Holistic healing also emphasizes the importance of self-care and self-awareness. It encourages individuals to take an active role in their healing journey by making conscious choices that support their well-being. This may involve adopting healthy lifestyle habits, such as regular exercise, a balanced diet, and adequate sleep. It may also involve cultivating positive relationships, engaging in stress-reducing activities, and practicing self-reflection and mindfulness.

By embracing holistic healing, individuals with mental health disorders can unlock their true potential for happiness and well-being. This approach recognizes that true healing goes beyond symptom management and requires a comprehensive understanding of the interconnectedness of the mind, body, and spirit. Through holistic healing, individuals can embark on a transformative journey towards greater self-awareness, self-empowerment, and lasting happiness.

Integrating Mind, Body, and Spirit

Integrating Mind, Body, and Spirit: A Path to Holistic Healing

In our fast-paced modern world, where stress and lifestyle diseases have become all too common, it is imperative that we adopt a holistic approach to healing mental health disorders. The subchapter titled "Integrating Mind, Body, and Spirit" in the book "Unlocking Happiness: A Holistic Approach to Healing Mental Health Disorders" explores the power of aligning these three fundamental aspects of our being. Regardless of your background or current situation, this chapter offers valuable insights and practical tools that can help you attain optimal wellness.

Our mental health is intricately connected to our physical health and spiritual well-being. When one aspect is out of balance, it can have a detrimental impact on the others. To achieve true healing, it is crucial to address the interconnectedness of mind, body, and spirit. This subchapter provides a comprehensive understanding of this connection and offers guidance on how to integrate these aspects into your daily life.

Through various exercises, meditation techniques, and mindful practices, you will learn how to listen to your body, identify and manage stress triggers, and cultivate a positive mindset. By developing a deeper awareness of your thoughts, emotions, and bodily sensations, you can gain valuable insights into the root causes of your mental health challenges. This integrated approach empowers you to take charge of your well-being and make conscious choices that support your healing journey.

The subchapter also delves into the importance of nurturing your spirit. It explores different spiritual practices, such as mindfulness, gratitude, and connection with nature, which can help you cultivate a sense of purpose, inner peace, and resilience. By tapping into your spiritual side, you can find solace, strength, and a deeper understanding of yourself.

Whether you are struggling with anxiety, depression, or any other mental health disorder, this subchapter provides a roadmap to holistic healing. It encourages you to embrace a lifestyle that nourishes your mind, body, and spirit, enabling you to unlock happiness and well-being from within.

Remember, you have the power to transform your life and overcome the challenges you face. By integrating mind, body, and spirit, you can embark on a transformative journey towards healing mental health disorders and living a fulfilling, vibrant life. Start your journey today and unlock the happiness that resides within you.

The Role of Nutrition in Mental Health

In today's fast-paced world, where stress and anxiety have become all too common, taking care of our mental health has become a top priority. While therapy and medication have long been the go-to solutions, an often overlooked aspect of mental health is nutrition. Proper nutrition plays a crucial role in maintaining a healthy mind and body. In this subchapter, we will delve into the profound impact of nutrition on mental health and explore how adopting a holistic approach can unlock happiness and heal mental health disorders.

When we think of nutrition, we often associate it with physical health and weight management. However, emerging research has shown that the food we consume has a direct impact on our brain chemistry and mental well-being. Our brain relies on a delicate balance of neurotransmitters, such as serotonin and dopamine, to regulate our mood and emotions. These neurotransmitters are made from the nutrients we obtain from our diet, including vitamins, minerals, and essential fatty acids.

A poor diet lacking in these crucial nutrients can disrupt the delicate balance, leading to mood swings, depression, anxiety, and even more severe mental health disorders. On the other hand, a diet rich in nutrients can promote optimal brain function, improve cognitive abilities, and protect against mental health disorders.

The modern Western diet, filled with processed foods, sugar, and unhealthy fats, has been linked to an increased risk of mental health disorders. Conversely, a diet centered around whole foods, such as fruits, vegetables, whole grains, lean proteins, and healthy fats, has been shown to have a protective effect on mental health. By nourishing our bodies with nutrient-dense foods, we provide the building blocks for optimal brain function and emotional well-being.

In this subchapter, we will explore the specific nutrients that play a vital role in mental health, such as omega-3 fatty acids, B vitamins, magnesium, and antioxidants. We will discuss how these nutrients impact brain health and provide practical tips on incorporating them into our daily diet.

Additionally, we will address the relationship between gut health and mental health. Emerging research has highlighted the importance of a healthy gut microbiome in maintaining optimal brain function. We will discuss the gut-brain axis and provide strategies to improve gut health through diet and lifestyle changes.

By understanding the profound impact of nutrition on mental health and adopting a holistic approach that combines therapy, medication, and a nutrient-rich diet, we can unlock happiness and heal mental health disorders. This subchapter aims to provide anyone interested in taking control of their mental well-being with the knowledge and tools needed to make informed choices about their nutrition and lifestyle, ultimately leading to a happier and healthier life.

Exercise and Physical Activity for Mental Well-being

In today's fast-paced world, where stress and anxiety have become commonplace, taking care of our mental health is more important than ever. While medications and therapy are valuable tools in treating mental health disorders, there is another powerful weapon that often goes unnoticed: exercise and physical activity.

The relationship between exercise and mental well-being is well-documented. Engaging in regular physical activity has been shown to have numerous benefits for our mental health, including reducing symptoms of depression and anxiety, improving overall mood, boosting self-esteem, and enhancing cognitive function. Exercise is not just beneficial for our physical health; it also has the power to transform our mental well-being.

When we exercise, our body releases endorphins, often referred to as "feel-good" hormones. These endorphins act as natural painkillers and mood elevators, helping to alleviate symptoms of stress and depression. Additionally, exercise increases the production of neurotransmitters like serotonin and dopamine, which play a crucial role in regulating our mood and emotions.

Physical activity also provides an opportunity for distraction and diversion from the daily stresses and worries that contribute to mental health disorders. Engaging in exercise allows us to shift our focus away from negative thoughts and rumination, providing a much-needed break for our mind. Whether it's going for a jog, practicing yoga, or hitting the gym, exercise offers a chance to escape the pressures of everyday life and find solace in the present moment.

Moreover, regular exercise has a profound impact on our self-esteem and body image. As we engage in physical activity and witness our bodies becoming stronger and more capable, we develop a sense of accomplishment and pride. This newfound confidence spills over into other areas of our life, empowering us to tackle challenges and overcome obstacles with greater resilience.

In the context of lifestyle diseases, exercise becomes even more crucial. Conditions such as obesity, diabetes, and cardiovascular diseases are closely linked to mental health disorders. By incorporating regular physical activity into our daily routine, we not only improve our physical health but also mitigate the risk of developing mental health issues associated with these lifestyle diseases. Exercise becomes a holistic approach to healing, addressing both the body and mind simultaneously.

In conclusion, exercise and physical activity are powerful tools for improving our mental well-being. Regardless of age or fitness level, anyone can benefit from incorporating regular exercise into their lifestyle. Whether it's taking a brisk walk, dancing, swimming, or engaging in team sports, finding an activity that brings joy and fulfillment is key. Let exercise be your prescription for unlocking happiness and healing mental health disorders.

The Power of Mindfulness and Meditation

In today's fast-paced world, where stress, anxiety, and depression have become rampant, it is crucial to find ways to heal our mental health disorders. While medical treatments and therapies are essential, there is a holistic approach that can greatly complement these efforts – the power of mindfulness and meditation.

Mindfulness is the practice of being fully present in the moment, without judgment or attachment to thoughts or emotions. It is about cultivating awareness and accepting whatever arises within us. Meditation, on the other hand, is a technique that helps us to train our minds and achieve a state of deep relaxation and inner peace.

When it comes to lifestyle diseases, such as heart disease, diabetes, and obesity, stress and unhealthy coping mechanisms often play a significant role. Mindfulness and meditation can be powerful tools in managing these conditions effectively.

Numerous studies have shown that regular practice of mindfulness and meditation can reduce stress levels and improve overall well-being. By focusing our attention on the present moment, we can detach ourselves from worries about the future or regrets about the past. This shift in mindset helps to alleviate stress and promotes a sense of calmness.

Furthermore, mindfulness and meditation can have a positive impact on our physical health. Research suggests that these practices can lower blood pressure, boost the immune system, and improve sleep quality. They also enhance our ability to make healthier lifestyle choices, such as eating nutritious food and engaging in regular physical activity.

In the context of mental health disorders, mindfulness and meditation can be transformative. They provide a natural means of managing symptoms like anxiety and depression. By observing our thoughts and emotions without judgment, we develop a greater understanding of our inner experiences. This self-awareness allows us to respond to challenging situations with more compassion and equanimity, reducing the intensity of negative emotions.

Moreover, mindfulness and meditation have the potential to rewire our brains. Studies using brain imaging technology have shown that these practices can increase the size of the prefrontal cortex, the area responsible for decision-making, emotional regulation, and empathy. This rewiring can lead to long-lasting changes in our mental and emotional well-being.

In conclusion, incorporating mindfulness and meditation into our lives can be a game-changer when it comes to healing mental health disorders and managing lifestyle diseases. By cultivating present-moment awareness and fostering a sense of inner peace, we can reduce stress, improve physical health, and enhance our overall well-being. So, whether you are struggling with a mental health disorder or seeking to prevent lifestyle diseases, the power of mindfulness and meditation is a practice worth exploring.

Creative Therapies for Mental Health

In today's fast-paced and stressful world, mental health disorders have become increasingly prevalent, affecting people from all walks of life. The impact of these disorders on individuals and their loved ones cannot be underestimated. However, there is hope. In the quest for healing mental health disorders, creative therapies have emerged as a powerful tool, offering a holistic approach that goes beyond traditional methods.

Unlocking Happiness: A Holistic Approach to Healing Mental Health Disorders introduces readers to the transformative power of creative therapies. This subchapter, "Creative Therapies for Mental Health," delves into the various techniques and practices that can be employed to promote mental well-being. Tailored to address the needs of anyone seeking a healthier and happier lifestyle, this subchapter offers insights and guidance on creative therapies specifically designed for mental health.

Art therapy is one such creative therapy that has gained recognition for its ability to tap into the subconscious and allow individuals to express their emotions and experiences visually. Through painting, drawing, or sculpting, individuals can gain a deeper understanding of their thoughts and feelings, providing a cathartic release and fostering personal growth.

Another powerful creative therapy is music therapy. Whether it's playing an instrument, singing, or simply listening to music, this therapy has been shown to reduce stress, improve mood, and enhance overall well-being. By harnessing the universal language of music, individuals can find solace, express themselves, and connect with their emotions in a profound way.

Dance and movement therapy is yet another creative approach that offers a unique way to integrate mind, body, and spirit. Through rhythmic movement and expression, individuals can release tension, improve body awareness, and boost self-esteem. Dance therapy can also foster connection and communication with others, promoting social well-being and reducing feelings of isolation.

Writing therapy, or journaling, is a creative outlet that allows individuals to explore their thoughts, emotions, and experiences through writing. This form of therapy provides a safe space for self-reflection, self-expression, and self-discovery. By putting thoughts and feelings onto paper, individuals can gain clarity, find healing, and develop a sense of empowerment.

Incorporating these creative therapies into one's lifestyle can not only complement traditional mental health treatments but also provide a unique and fulfilling way to promote mental well-being. Unlocking Happiness: A Holistic Approach to Healing Mental Health Disorders offers practical advice, exercises, and resources to guide readers on their journey towards unlocking happiness and finding solace through creative therapies. Regardless of one's background or lifestyle, these creative therapies offer a beacon of hope, inviting individuals to embark on a transformative path towards mental well-being.

Connecting with Nature for Healing

In today's fast-paced and technology-driven world, it is easy to become disconnected from nature. We spend most of our days indoors, surrounded by artificial lights and immersed in digital screens. However, research has shown that reconnecting with nature can have profound healing effects on our mental and physical well-being. In this subchapter, we will explore the power of nature in healing lifestyle diseases and how you can harness its benefits to unlock happiness and improve your overall health.

Nature has an innate ability to calm our minds and rejuvenate our bodies. When we immerse ourselves in natural surroundings, we experience a sense of peace and tranquility that is often lacking in our urban lifestyles. Studies have indicated that spending time in nature can reduce stress, anxiety, and depression, as well as boost our mood and increase feelings of happiness. Nature acts as a natural stress reliever, allowing us to escape the pressures of daily life and find solace in its beauty.

Moreover, connecting with nature can also have a positive impact on our physical health, particularly in relation to lifestyle diseases. Conditions such as obesity, diabetes, and heart disease are often a result of sedentary lifestyles and poor dietary choices. By spending time outdoors and engaging in activities such as walking, hiking, or gardening, we can incorporate physical exercise into our routine and improve our overall fitness levels. Additionally, being in nature exposes us to fresh air and natural sunlight, which are essential for our body's optimal functioning and immune system support.

To fully harness the healing power of nature, it is important to engage all our senses. Take a moment to breathe in the fresh scent of the forest, listen to the soothing sounds of birds chirping, feel the warmth of sunlight on your skin, and observe the intricate details of a flower. By consciously immersing ourselves in these sensory experiences, we can deepen our connection with nature and enhance its healing effects.

Incorporating nature into our daily lives does not necessarily require extensive time or resources. Simple activities such as taking a walk in the park, tending to a small garden, or even opening a window to let fresh air in can make a significant difference. It's about finding moments of connection with the natural world amidst our busy lives.

In conclusion, reconnecting with nature is a powerful tool for healing lifestyle diseases and promoting overall well-being. By immersing ourselves in its beauty and engaging our senses, we can reduce stress, improve our mood, enhance physical fitness, and unlock happiness. So, take a step outside, breathe in the natural world, and let nature be your guide on the path to healing.

Chapter 3: Unlocking Happiness: Tools for Healing

Seeking Professional Help

In the journey towards unlocking happiness and achieving a holistic approach to healing mental health disorders, seeking professional help plays a vital role. Whether you are struggling with stress, anxiety, depression, or any other mental health issue, reaching out to a qualified professional can provide you with the support and guidance you need.

The world we live in today is fast-paced and demanding, leading to an increase in lifestyle diseases. These conditions often go hand in hand with mental health disorders, further exacerbating the challenges individuals face. However, it is important to remember that seeking professional help is not a sign of weakness but rather a courageous step towards taking control of your well-being.

A mental health professional, such as a therapist, counselor, or psychiatrist, can offer you valuable insights and strategies that can help you navigate through life's difficulties. They possess the knowledge and expertise required to evaluate your condition, provide an accurate diagnosis, and recommend appropriate treatment options. By working with these professionals, you can gain a deeper understanding of your mental health, develop coping mechanisms, and establish a personalized plan to address your specific needs.

One of the primary benefits of seeking professional help is the opportunity to engage in therapy. Therapy offers a safe and confidential space for individuals to express their thoughts and emotions freely. Through various therapeutic techniques, such as cognitive-behavioral therapy (CBT) or mindfulness-based stress reduction (MBSR), you can learn to identify negative thinking patterns, manage stress, and develop healthier ways of coping.

Additionally, mental health professionals can provide medication management if necessary. In some cases, lifestyle diseases may require pharmacological interventions to alleviate symptoms and restore balance. It is essential to remember that medication alone is not a cure but can be a useful tool when combined with therapy and other holistic practices.

Moreover, seeking professional help can also help you build a support network. Mental health professionals can connect you with support groups, workshops, and resources within your community. These networks can provide a sense of belonging, understanding, and encouragement as you navigate your healing journey.

Remember, seeking professional help is not a sign of defeat, but rather a proactive step towards regaining control of your life and unlocking happiness. Whether you are struggling with a lifestyle disease or any other mental health disorder, reaching out for help is a courageous decision that can lead to transformative change. Embrace the opportunity to work with a professional who can guide you towards a healthier and happier future.

Therapeutic Approaches for Mental Health Disorders

In today's fast-paced and stressful world, mental health disorders have become increasingly prevalent, affecting individuals of all ages and backgrounds. These disorders, often referred to as lifestyle diseases, can severely impact a person's overall well-being and quality of life. However, there is hope. With the right therapeutic approaches, these disorders can be effectively managed and even overcome.

"Unlocking Happiness: A Holistic Approach to Healing Mental Health Disorders" aims to provide a comprehensive guide for anyone seeking to understand and address their mental health concerns. This subchapter, "Therapeutic Approaches for Mental Health Disorders," explores various strategies and techniques that can aid in the healing process.

One of the key therapeutic approaches discussed in this subchapter is cognitive-behavioral therapy (CBT). CBT focuses on identifying and challenging negative thought patterns and behaviors that contribute to mental health disorders. By learning to reframe thoughts and adopt healthier coping mechanisms, individuals can experience significant improvements in their mental well-being.

Another approach explored is mindfulness and meditation. These practices encourage individuals to be fully present in the moment, cultivating a sense of calm and awareness. Mindfulness has been proven to reduce stress, anxiety, and depression, making it an invaluable tool for managing mental health disorders.

Additionally, alternative therapies such as art therapy, music therapy, and animal-assisted therapy are discussed. These approaches utilize creative expression, music, and interaction with animals to promote emotional healing and self-discovery. These non-traditional methods can be particularly beneficial for individuals who struggle with traditional talk therapies.

Finally, lifestyle modifications are explored as an essential aspect of therapeutic approaches for mental health disorders.

This subchapter emphasizes the importance of regular exercise, a balanced diet, and sufficient sleep in maintaining good mental health. It also delves into the significance of social support systems and healthy relationships in the healing process.

"Unlocking Happiness: A Holistic Approach to Healing Mental Health Disorders" aims to empower readers with the knowledge and tools they need to effectively manage their mental health. By adopting a holistic perspective and incorporating a range of therapeutic approaches, individuals can unlock their happiness and reclaim control over their lives. Whether you are struggling with a mental health disorder or seeking to support a loved one, this subchapter provides invaluable insights and strategies to facilitate healing and well-being.

Cognitive Behavioral Therapy (CBT)

In today's fast-paced world, where stress, anxiety, and depression have become a part of our everyday lives, it's crucial to explore effective methods for healing mental health disorders. One such approach that has gained immense popularity is Cognitive Behavioral Therapy (CBT). This subchapter aims to provide an understanding of CBT and its role in addressing lifestyle diseases.

CBT is a form of psychotherapy that focuses on the connection between thoughts, feelings, and behaviors. It recognizes that our thoughts influence our emotions and ultimately affect our actions. By identifying and challenging negative thought patterns, CBT helps individuals develop healthier beliefs and behaviors, leading to improved mental well-being.

CBT offers a holistic approach to healing mental health disorders, as it addresses both the cognitive and behavioral aspects of a person's life. It enables individuals to gain insight into their thinking patterns and helps them make positive changes in their behavior. By doing so, CBT empowers individuals to break free from the cycle of negative thoughts and self-destructive behaviors that contribute to lifestyle diseases.

One of the key principles of CBT is recognizing and challenging cognitive distortions. These are irrational thoughts that often lead to negative emotions and maladaptive behaviors. Through various techniques, such as cognitive restructuring and reframing, individuals learn to identify these distortions and replace them with more realistic and positive thoughts. This cognitive shift can have a profound impact on their emotional well-being and overall quality of life.

Furthermore, CBT focuses on behavioral changes that contribute to lifestyle diseases. It encourages individuals to engage in activities that promote their well-being, such as regular exercise, healthy eating, and stress-reduction techniques. By incorporating these behaviors into their daily lives, individuals can experience a significant improvement in their mental health and reduce the risk of lifestyle diseases.

CBT is a collaborative and goal-oriented therapy that empowers individuals to take an active role in their healing journey. It equips them with practical skills and tools to manage their thoughts, emotions, and behaviors effectively. By providing a comprehensive approach to mental health disorders, CBT offers hope and a path towards unlocking happiness and well-being.

Whether you're struggling with stress, anxiety, or depression, or simply seeking ways to improve your mental health, CBT is a valuable tool. By understanding the connection between your thoughts, feelings, and behaviors, you can take control of your well-being and work towards a happier and healthier life.

Dialectical Behavior Therapy (DBT)

Dialectical Behavior Therapy (DBT): Unlocking Happiness and Healing Mental Health Disorders

In today's fast-paced and stress-inducing world, mental health disorders have become an increasingly prevalent issue. From anxiety and depression to personality disorders and addiction, the impact of these conditions on our overall well-being cannot be understated. However, hope lies in the form of Dialectical Behavior Therapy (DBT), a revolutionary treatment approach that offers a holistic path towards healing.

DBT, developed by renowned psychologist Marsha M. Linehan, is a comprehensive therapy that combines elements of cognitive-behavioral therapy, mindfulness, and acceptance-based strategies. It aims to empower individuals by providing them with the necessary skills to manage emotions, navigate relationships, and cope with life's challenges effectively.

This subchapter of "Unlocking Happiness: A Holistic Approach to Healing Mental Health Disorders" explores the transformative power of DBT for individuals suffering from lifestyle diseases. Whether you're struggling with chronic stress, addiction, or any other condition impacting your mental well-being, DBT offers practical tools to help you regain control and find happiness.

One of the key pillars of DBT is mindfulness, which involves paying attention to the present moment without judgment. By cultivating mindfulness, individuals can develop greater self-awareness, reduce emotional reactivity, and enhance their ability to make conscious choices. This practice is particularly valuable for those dealing with lifestyle diseases, as it can help break harmful patterns and develop healthier habits.

DBT also focuses on interpersonal effectiveness, teaching individuals effective communication, boundary setting, and conflict resolution skills. These skills are essential for managing relationships, reducing stress, and maintaining a balanced lifestyle. By improving interpersonal effectiveness, DBT empowers individuals to build healthier connections and create a support system that contributes to their overall well-being.

Furthermore, DBT offers specific strategies for emotion regulation, helping individuals identify and manage intense emotions in healthy ways. This is particularly relevant for those experiencing lifestyle diseases, as emotional dysregulation often exacerbates symptoms and impedes progress. By learning to regulate emotions effectively, individuals can reduce stress, improve decision-making, and enhance their overall quality of life.

In conclusion, Dialectical Behavior Therapy (DBT) offers a comprehensive and holistic approach to healing mental health disorders, including those associated with lifestyle diseases. By integrating mindfulness, interpersonal effectiveness, and emotion regulation skills, DBT equips individuals with the tools they need to navigate life's challenges and unlock happiness. Whether you are struggling with chronic stress, addiction, or any other condition impacting your mental well-being, DBT can guide you towards a path of healing and transform your life for the better.

Acceptance and Commitment Therapy (ACT)

Acceptance and Commitment Therapy (ACT) is a powerful approach to healing mental health disorders that can benefit anyone, especially those dealing with lifestyle diseases. In this subchapter, we will explore the core principles and techniques of ACT, providing you with a holistic approach to unlocking happiness and promoting mental well-being.

ACT is based on the idea that suffering is a natural part of life, and instead of trying to eliminate or control our negative thoughts and emotions, we should learn to accept them. By accepting our thoughts and feelings, we can create a space for healing and growth. ACT teaches us to embrace the present moment, regardless of the challenges we face, and to commit to taking positive action towards our values and goals.

One of the key concepts in ACT is mindfulness. Mindfulness is the practice of paying attention to the present moment without judgment. By cultivating mindfulness, we can increase our awareness of our thoughts and emotions, allowing us to respond to them in a more compassionate and effective way. Mindfulness can help us develop a greater sense of self-awareness, reduce stress, and improve our overall well-being.

Another important aspect of ACT is the identification of our values. Values are what give our lives meaning and purpose. By clarifying our values, we can align our actions with what truly matters to us, leading to a more fulfilling and satisfying life. ACT encourages us to set goals that are in line with our values and to take committed action towards achieving them.

ACT also teaches us to defuse from our thoughts. Often, our thoughts can be unhelpful and lead to suffering. ACT helps us to recognize that thoughts are just words or mental events, and they do not define us. By learning to defuse from our thoughts, we can create distance and perspective, reducing their impact on our well-being.

In conclusion, Acceptance and Commitment Therapy (ACT) offers a holistic approach to healing mental health disorders and can benefit anyone, especially those dealing with lifestyle diseases. By embracing acceptance, mindfulness, values, and defusion, we can unlock happiness and promote mental well-being. ACT empowers us to live a meaningful life, even in the face of challenges, and encourages us to take committed action towards our values and goals. So, if you are seeking a powerful approach to healing mental health disorders and improving your overall well-being, ACT is a valuable tool to explore.

Self-Care Practices for Mental Well-being

In today's fast-paced world, where stress and anxiety are pervasive, taking care of our mental well-being has become more important than ever. The way we care for our minds and emotions greatly impacts our overall happiness and quality of life. This subchapter explores a range of self-care practices that can help individuals combat lifestyle diseases and improve their mental well-being.

1. Mindfulness and Meditation: Engaging in mindfulness and meditation practices can help individuals develop a greater awareness of their thoughts and emotions. By focusing on the present moment and letting go of judgement, individuals can reduce stress, improve concentration, and cultivate a sense of calm and inner peace.

2. Regular Exercise: Physical activity is not only beneficial for our physical health but also plays a vital role in maintaining good mental well-being. Engaging in regular exercise releases endorphins, which boost mood and reduce symptoms of anxiety and depression. Activities such as walking, yoga, or dancing can be incorporated into daily routines to promote mental well-being.

3. Adequate Sleep: Sleep is essential for our mental and physical health. Lack of sleep can lead to increased stress levels, decreased cognitive function, and impaired emotional well-being. Practicing good sleep hygiene, such as establishing a regular sleep schedule and creating a relaxing bedtime routine, can greatly improve mental well-being.

4. Nurturing Relationships: Building and maintaining strong relationships is crucial for our mental health. Connecting with loved ones, friends, and even pets can provide emotional support, reduce feelings of loneliness, and enhance overall happiness. Engaging in activities that foster healthy social connections, such as joining clubs or volunteering, can also promote mental well-being.

5. Healthy Diet: The food we consume can greatly impact our mental well-being. A balanced diet rich in fruits, vegetables, whole grains, and lean proteins provides essential nutrients for brain health. Avoiding excessive consumption of processed foods, caffeine, and alcohol can also contribute to maintaining stable mood and mental well-being.

6. Stress Management Techniques: Chronic stress can take a toll on mental well-being and contribute to lifestyle diseases. Incorporating stress management techniques such as deep breathing exercises, journaling, or engaging in hobbies can help individuals effectively manage and reduce stress levels.

By incorporating these self-care practices into your daily routine, you can take proactive steps towards improving your mental well-being. Remember, self-care is not selfish but necessary for leading a fulfilling and happy life. Embracing these practices can unlock happiness and provide a holistic approach to healing mental health disorders.

Establishing a Daily Routine

In our fast-paced and hectic lives, it is easy to overlook the importance of establishing a daily routine. However, a carefully crafted routine can be a powerful tool in managing and preventing lifestyle diseases, while also promoting overall well-being and happiness. This subchapter will explore the significance of a daily routine and provide practical tips on how to build one that suits your needs.

Modern lifestyles have given rise to an array of lifestyle diseases such as obesity, diabetes, heart disease, and mental health disorders. These conditions not only threaten our physical health but also take a toll on our mental and emotional well-being. Establishing a daily routine can help counteract these negative effects by providing structure and stability to our lives.

A well-designed routine can ensure that we prioritize activities that promote good health. This includes allocating time for exercise, meal planning, and relaxation techniques like meditation or mindfulness. By incorporating these activities into our daily lives, we can reduce the risk of lifestyle diseases and enhance our overall quality of life.

Moreover, maintaining a consistent routine can help manage stress, anxiety, and depression. When our lives are filled with uncertainty and chaos, it can be challenging to find a sense of stability and control. A daily routine provides a framework that allows us to regain a sense of purpose and direction. It creates a sense of predictability and certainty, which can be incredibly soothing to our mental health.

To establish a daily routine that works for you, it is essential to consider your individual needs and preferences. Start by identifying the activities that are most important for your well-being and prioritize them in your routine. Experiment with different schedules and be flexible in adapting to unforeseen circumstances. Remember, it is not about perfection but rather finding a routine that supports your mental and physical health.

In conclusion, establishing a daily routine is a crucial step in managing and preventing lifestyle diseases while promoting overall happiness and well-being. By incorporating activities that support our health and mental well-being, we can create a sense of stability and control in our lives. So, take a moment to reflect on your current routine and make the necessary adjustments to unlock the key to a healthier and happier future.

Practicing Gratitude

In today's fast-paced and stressful world, it's easy to get caught up in the whirlwind of our daily lives and forget about the simple pleasures that bring us joy. However, cultivating an attitude of gratitude can have a transformative effect on our overall well-being, especially when it comes to managing lifestyle diseases. In this subchapter, we will explore the power of gratitude and how it can contribute to healing mental health disorders.

Gratitude is more than just saying "thank you." It's a mindset, a way of looking at the world with appreciation and recognizing the positive aspects of our lives. When we practice gratitude regularly, we shift our focus from what's lacking to what we have, fostering a sense of abundance and contentment.

Research has shown that incorporating gratitude into our daily lives can have a significant impact on mental health. It has been linked to increased happiness, improved self-esteem, reduced stress levels, and enhanced overall well-being. For those struggling with lifestyle diseases, such as anxiety or depression, practicing gratitude can provide a valuable coping mechanism and support their healing journey.

One simple way to start cultivating gratitude is by keeping a gratitude journal. Each day, take a few moments to reflect on the things you are grateful for and write them down. It could be as simple as appreciating a beautiful sunset, a supportive friend, or a delicious meal. As you make this a daily habit, you'll begin to notice a shift in your mindset and an increased awareness of the positive aspects of your life.

Another powerful practice is expressing gratitude to others. Take the time to thank those who have made a positive impact on your life, whether it's a loved one, a colleague, or even a stranger who showed kindness. This act of appreciation not only strengthens your relationships but also deepens your sense of connection and gratitude.

Additionally, incorporating mindfulness into your gratitude practice can amplify its benefits. By being fully present in the moment and savoring the experiences that bring you joy, you enhance your ability to appreciate them fully.

Remember, practicing gratitude is a lifelong journey, and it may take time to rewire your brain to focus on the positive. However, the effort is well worth it. By embracing gratitude, you can unlock happiness and harness its healing power, contributing to the management and improvement of lifestyle diseases.

So, take a moment today to pause and reflect on the countless blessings in your life. Cultivate an attitude of gratitude, and watch as it transforms your mental health and overall well-being.

Cultivating Healthy Relationships

In today's fast-paced and digitally connected world, it has become increasingly important to cultivate healthy relationships in order to maintain our overall well-being. Relationships play a crucial role in our lives, affecting our mental and emotional health, and even contributing to the development of lifestyle diseases. In this subchapter, we will explore the significance of healthy relationships and discover strategies to foster and nurture them.

Healthy relationships are essential for our overall happiness and mental well-being. Research has consistently shown that individuals with strong social connections are more likely to experience lower levels of stress, depression, and anxiety. On the other hand, a lack of healthy relationships can lead to feelings of isolation, loneliness, and even contribute to the development of lifestyle diseases such as cardiovascular conditions, obesity, and diabetes.

To cultivate healthy relationships, it is important to prioritize both quality and quantity. Quality relationships are built on trust, respect, and effective communication. It is crucial to surround yourself with individuals who support and uplift you, rather than those who drain your energy or bring negativity into your life. Additionally, maintaining a balance between your personal and professional life is essential to prevent burnout and ensure you have enough time and energy to dedicate to your relationships.

Effective communication is the cornerstone of healthy relationships. Active listening, empathy, and understanding play pivotal roles in nurturing connections. It is important to express your thoughts and emotions openly and honestly, while also being receptive to the needs and concerns of others. By fostering a safe and non-judgmental space for communication, you can strengthen your relationships and resolve conflicts constructively.

Another vital aspect of cultivating healthy relationships is self-care. Taking care of your physical, mental, and emotional well-being is crucial for being able to give and receive love and support. Prioritizing activities that bring you joy and practicing self-compassion not only enhance your overall well-being but also enable you to show up fully in your relationships.

In conclusion, cultivating healthy relationships is an integral part of leading a happy and fulfilling life. By prioritizing quality relationships, effective communication, and self-care, we can protect ourselves from the negative impacts of isolation and loneliness and support our mental health. Building and nurturing these relationships can help us combat lifestyle diseases and unlock happiness in our lives.

Setting Boundaries and Managing Stress

In today's fast-paced world, it is becoming increasingly important to set boundaries and effectively manage stress in order to maintain good mental health. This subchapter aims to provide practical strategies and techniques to help anyone, especially those dealing with lifestyle diseases, unlock happiness and find a holistic approach to healing mental health disorders.

Setting boundaries is crucial for maintaining healthy relationships, whether it be with friends, family, or colleagues. By clearly defining what is acceptable and what is not, individuals can protect their mental well-being and prevent unnecessary stress. Learning to say "no" when necessary and prioritizing self-care are crucial steps in setting boundaries. It is essential to recognize that it is not selfish to prioritize one's mental health and well-being, as it ultimately allows individuals to become more present and engaged in their relationships and responsibilities.

Managing stress is another vital aspect of achieving good mental health. Lifestyle diseases often exacerbate stress levels, making it even more crucial to find effective coping mechanisms. One technique is to identify stress triggers and develop personalized stress management strategies. This may include practicing mindfulness and meditation, engaging in regular exercise, or pursuing creative outlets such as painting or writing. Finding what works best for each individual is key, as everyone has unique needs and preferences.

In addition to individual strategies, creating a supportive environment is also essential. Surrounding oneself with positive and understanding individuals can greatly alleviate stress levels. Seeking professional help, such as therapy or counseling, can also provide valuable guidance and support in managing stress and setting boundaries.

It is important to remember that healing mental health disorders requires a holistic approach. This means addressing not only the symptoms but also the underlying causes and contributing factors. By incorporating lifestyle changes such as a balanced diet, regular exercise, and quality sleep into one's routine, individuals can enhance their overall well-being and reduce the risk of lifestyle diseases.

In conclusion, setting boundaries and managing stress are vital components of maintaining good mental health, especially for individuals dealing with lifestyle diseases. By prioritizing self-care, seeking support, and implementing effective stress management strategies, anyone can unlock happiness and find a holistic approach to healing mental health disorders. Remember, it is never too late to make positive changes and prioritize your well-being.

Holistic Approaches to Medication and Alternative Treatments

In the modern world, lifestyle diseases have become increasingly prevalent, affecting individuals of all ages and backgrounds. These disorders, ranging from anxiety and depression to chronic stress and insomnia, can greatly impact our overall well-being and quality of life. While conventional medication has long been the go-to solution for treating such conditions, it is essential to consider holistic approaches and alternative treatments to unlock happiness and heal mental health disorders more effectively.

Holistic medicine focuses on treating the whole person rather than just the symptoms, taking into account the interconnectedness of the mind, body, and spirit. By addressing all aspects of an individual's life, including emotional, physical, and environmental factors, holistic approaches aim to promote optimal health and well-being. When it comes to lifestyle diseases, this approach proves to be particularly beneficial.

One key aspect of holistic medicine is the incorporation of alternative treatments alongside or instead of conventional medication. These treatments include various techniques, such as acupuncture, aromatherapy, herbal medicine, meditation, and yoga. These alternative therapies have gained recognition for their ability to alleviate symptoms, reduce stress, and improve overall mental health.

Acupuncture, for instance, involves the stimulation of specific points on the body using thin needles, promoting the flow of energy and restoring balance within. Aromatherapy utilizes essential oils to create a soothing and calming environment, aiding in relaxation and reducing anxiety. Herbal medicine, on the other hand, harnesses the healing properties of plants to treat various ailments, including mental health disorders.

Meditation and yoga are powerful practices that help individuals connect with their inner selves, cultivate mindfulness, and manage stress. Through deep breathing exercises, mindfulness meditation allows individuals to observe their thoughts and emotions without judgment, promoting a sense of peace and tranquility. Similarly, yoga combines physical postures, breathing techniques, and meditation to improve mental and physical well-being.

While these alternative treatments may not completely replace conventional medication, they offer valuable adjunctive therapies that can enhance overall treatment outcomes. Integrating holistic approaches and alternative treatments into a comprehensive treatment plan for lifestyle diseases provides individuals with a well-rounded and personalized approach to healing mental health disorders.

In conclusion, when it comes to addressing lifestyle diseases, a holistic approach to medication and alternative treatments proves to be a valuable strategy. By considering the interconnectedness of the mind, body, and spirit, individuals can unlock happiness and promote healing. Incorporating practices such as acupuncture, aromatherapy, herbal medicine, meditation, and yoga alongside conventional medication provides a comprehensive approach to mental health treatment, ultimately leading to improved well-being and a more fulfilling life.

Chapter 4: Overcoming Depression

Understanding Depression: Causes and Symptoms

Depression is a complex and pervasive mental health disorder that affects millions of people worldwide. In this subchapter, we will explore the causes and symptoms of depression, shedding light on this often misunderstood condition. Whether you have experienced depression personally or know someone who has, this information will provide valuable insights into understanding and managing this debilitating illness.

Causes of Depression:

Depression does not have a single cause and can arise from a combination of factors. Biological factors, such as genetics and imbalances in brain chemistry, can contribute to the development of depression. Additionally, certain life events, such as trauma, loss, or major changes, can trigger or exacerbate depressive episodes. Other factors, including chronic illness, substance abuse, or a family history of depression, can also increase the risk.

Symptoms of Depression:

Recognizing the symptoms of depression is essential for early intervention and effective treatment. While everyone's experience with depression can vary, common symptoms include persistent feelings of sadness, hopelessness, and emptiness. Individuals with depression often lose interest in activities they once enjoyed, experience changes in appetite and sleep patterns, and struggle with concentration and decision-making. Physical symptoms, such as fatigue, headaches, or digestive issues, may also accompany depression.

Understanding the Link to Lifestyle Diseases:

Depression is often categorized as a lifestyle disease due to its close association with various lifestyle factors. Research suggests that an unhealthy lifestyle, including poor nutrition, lack of exercise, chronic stress, and inadequate sleep, can increase the risk of developing depression. Conversely, engaging in a healthy lifestyle that prioritizes balanced nutrition, regular exercise, stress reduction techniques, and sufficient rest can promote mental well-being and reduce the likelihood of depression.

Taking a Holistic Approach:

Addressing depression requires a holistic approach that considers both biological and lifestyle factors. While medication and therapy are essential components of treatment, lifestyle modifications can also play a pivotal role in managing depression. By adopting healthy habits, individuals can improve their overall well-being and reduce the severity and frequency of depressive episodes.

In conclusion, understanding the causes and symptoms of depression is crucial for anyone seeking to support their own mental health or that of others. By recognizing the link between depression and lifestyle diseases, individuals can take proactive steps towards prevention and management. With a holistic approach to healing, it is possible to unlock happiness and regain control over mental health disorders like depression.

Traditional Treatments for Depression

Depression is a debilitating mental health disorder that affects millions of people worldwide. While modern medicine and therapy have made significant advancements in treating depression, traditional treatments have also played a crucial role in alleviating symptoms and promoting overall well-being. In this subchapter, we will explore some of the traditional treatments for depression that have been used for centuries, offering a holistic approach to healing mental health disorders.

One of the most widely recognized traditional treatments for depression is herbal medicine. Various herbs, such as St. John's Wort and saffron, have been used for centuries to alleviate symptoms of depression. These natural remedies work by targeting neurotransmitters in the brain, helping to regulate mood and reduce feelings of sadness and hopelessness. However, it is important to consult with a healthcare professional before incorporating herbal medicine into your treatment plan, as they can interact with other medications.

Another traditional treatment for depression is acupuncture. Originating from ancient Chinese medicine, acupuncture involves the insertion of thin needles into specific points on the body. This practice aims to restore the flow of energy and balance the body's systems. Studies have shown that acupuncture can help reduce symptoms of depression by stimulating the release of endorphins, the body's natural painkillers, and promoting relaxation.

In addition to herbal medicine and acupuncture, traditional practices like mindfulness and meditation have gained recognition in the treatment of depression. These practices involve focusing one's attention on the present moment, cultivating self-acceptance, and developing a sense of inner peace. By incorporating mindfulness and meditation into daily routines, individuals can learn to manage stress, reduce anxiety, and improve overall mental well-being.

Furthermore, engaging in physical activities, such as yoga or Tai Chi, can also be beneficial in treating depression. These practices combine gentle movements with deep breathing exercises, promoting relaxation, and the release of endorphins. Regular physical activity has been shown to improve mood, increase energy levels, and reduce symptoms of depression.

While these traditional treatments for depression can be effective, it is important to remember that everyone's journey to recovery is unique. It is crucial to work with a healthcare professional to determine the best treatment plan for your individual needs. By embracing a holistic approach and incorporating traditional treatments into your lifestyle, you can unlock happiness and promote healing from within.

In conclusion, traditional treatments for depression offer an alternative approach to healing mental health disorders. Herbal medicine, acupuncture, mindfulness, meditation, and physical activities such as yoga and Tai Chi have been used for centuries to alleviate symptoms of depression and promote overall well-being. By incorporating these practices into your lifestyle, you can take a holistic approach to mental health, unlocking happiness and finding inner peace.

Holistic Approaches to Managing Depression

In today's fast-paced world, where stress and anxiety levels are constantly on the rise, it is not surprising that mental health disorders such as depression have become prevalent. Depression can have a profound impact on an individual's overall well-being, affecting their emotional, physical, and mental health. While traditional treatments such as medication and therapy have proven to be effective, there is a growing recognition of the importance of holistic approaches in managing depression.

Holistic approaches to managing depression focus on treating the whole person rather than just the symptoms. These approaches recognize that mental health disorders are often interconnected with other aspects of our lives, such as our lifestyle choices, diet, and social support systems. By addressing these underlying factors, individuals can experience long-lasting relief from depressive symptoms and improve their overall quality of life.

One of the key aspects of a holistic approach to managing depression is lifestyle modification. Engaging in regular physical activity, practicing mindfulness and meditation, and incorporating stress management techniques into daily routines can all have a positive impact on mental health. Exercise releases endorphins, which are known as "feel-good" hormones, promoting a sense of well-being and reducing depressive symptoms. Mindfulness and meditation help individuals develop a greater sense of self-awareness, allowing them to better manage their emotions and thoughts.

Another important aspect of managing depression holistically is nutrition. Research has shown a strong link between diet and mental health, with certain foods promoting brain health and others exacerbating depressive symptoms. A diet rich in whole foods, such as fruits, vegetables, whole grains, and lean proteins, can provide the necessary nutrients to support brain function and improve mood. Avoiding processed foods, excessive sugar, and caffeine is also recommended, as they can contribute to mood swings and energy crashes.

Additionally, holistic approaches to managing depression emphasize the importance of building a strong support network. Surrounding oneself with positive and understanding individuals can provide a sense of belonging and reduce feelings of isolation. Participating in support groups, seeking therapy, and maintaining healthy relationships are all crucial for managing depression effectively.

In conclusion, holistic approaches to managing depression offer a comprehensive and integrated approach to mental health care. By addressing lifestyle factors, nutrition, and social support, individuals can take an active role in their own healing process. While medication and therapy can be effective, incorporating holistic practices can provide individuals with long-term strategies to manage and prevent depressive symptoms. By adopting a holistic approach, anyone can unlock happiness and improve their mental well-being, leading to a healthier, happier life.

Lifestyle Changes for Depression Management

Depression is a complex mental health disorder that affects millions of people worldwide. While medication and therapy are often essential components of treatment, lifestyle changes can also play a significant role in managing and alleviating symptoms of depression. In this subchapter, we will explore various lifestyle changes that can help individuals on their journey to unlocking happiness and healing their mental health.

1. Exercise: Engaging in regular physical activity has been scientifically proven to boost mood and reduce symptoms of depression. Exercise stimulates the release of endorphins, the body's natural feel-good chemicals, which can result in improved well-being and reduced stress. Incorporating activities like walking, jogging, yoga, or dancing into your daily routine can have a profound impact on your mental health.

2. Balanced Diet: The food we consume directly affects our physical and mental well-being. A diet rich in whole grains, fruits, vegetables, lean proteins, and healthy fats can provide essential nutrients and improve brain function. Avoiding processed foods, excessive sugar, caffeine, and alcohol can help stabilize mood and energy levels, promoting better mental health.

3. Sleep Hygiene: Good quality sleep is crucial for overall mental health. Establishing a consistent sleep schedule, practicing relaxation techniques before bed, and creating a peaceful sleep environment can contribute to restorative sleep. Lack of sleep can exacerbate symptoms of depression, so prioritizing sleep hygiene is essential.

4. Stress Management: Chronic stress can worsen depressive symptoms. Finding healthy ways to manage stress, such as practicing mindfulness, deep breathing exercises, or engaging in hobbies and activities you enjoy, can help reduce stress levels and promote emotional well-being.

5. Social Connections: Isolation and loneliness can intensify feelings of depression. Cultivating strong social connections,

whether through friends, family, or support groups, can provide emotional support and a sense of belonging. Engaging in social activities and fostering meaningful relationships can significantly contribute to improved mental health.

6. Self-Care: Taking care of your emotional, physical, and spiritual needs is crucial in managing depression. Engaging in self-care activities that bring you joy and relaxation, such as reading, taking baths, practicing meditation, or pursuing hobbies, can help maintain a positive mindset and boost overall well-being.

Remember that everyone's journey with depression is unique. It is essential to consult with a healthcare professional to create a personalized treatment plan that incorporates lifestyle changes alongside therapy and medication. By implementing these lifestyle changes, individuals can take proactive steps towards managing their depression, promoting mental well-being, and unlocking happiness in their lives.

Natural Remedies for Depression

Depression, a common mental health disorder affecting millions of people worldwide, can often be debilitating and overwhelming. While medical treatments and therapy are essential for managing depression, there are also natural remedies that can complement traditional approaches. In this subchapter, we will explore various natural remedies for depression, offering a holistic approach to healing mental health disorders.

1. Exercise: Physical activity has been proven to boost serotonin levels, a neurotransmitter responsible for regulating mood. Engaging in regular exercise, whether it be walking, jogging, or practicing yoga, can help alleviate symptoms of depression and improve overall well-being.

2. Healthy Diet: The food we consume plays a significant role in our mental health. Incorporating a balanced diet rich in fruits, vegetables, whole grains, and lean proteins can provide essential nutrients that promote brain health. Additionally, certain foods like fatty fish, walnuts, and dark chocolate contain omega-3 fatty acids and antioxidants that have been linked to reducing symptoms of depression.

3. Herbal Remedies: Several herbal remedies have shown promise in managing depression. St. John's Wort, for example, has been used for centuries to alleviate symptoms of mild to moderate depression. However, it is crucial to consult with a healthcare professional before incorporating any herbal supplements, as they can interact with prescription medications.

4. Mindfulness and Meditation: Practicing mindfulness and meditation techniques can help individuals gain control over their thoughts and emotions. These practices promote relaxation, reduce stress, and improve overall mental well-being. Mindfulness-based therapies, such as Mindfulness-Based Cognitive Therapy (MBCT), have been found to be effective in preventing relapses of depression.

5. Essential Oils: Aromatherapy using essential oils like lavender, chamomile, and bergamot can have a calming effect on the mind and body. These oils can be used in diffusers, bath salts, or massage oils to promote relaxation and reduce anxiety, ultimately aiding in the management of depression.

It is important to note that while these natural remedies can be beneficial, they should not replace professional medical advice or treatment. Each individual's experience with depression is unique, and what works for one person may not work for another. Therefore, it is crucial to consult with a healthcare professional to develop a comprehensive treatment plan that addresses personal needs and circumstances.

By incorporating these natural remedies into one's lifestyle, individuals can take proactive steps towards managing depression and improving overall mental health. Unlocking happiness is within reach, and a holistic approach that addresses both medical and natural remedies can empower individuals to take control of their mental well-being.

Supportive Therapies for Depression

Depression is a prevalent mental health disorder that affects millions of people worldwide. While medication and psychotherapy are commonly used treatment options, there are also several supportive therapies that can significantly contribute to alleviating symptoms and promoting overall mental well-being. In this subchapter, we will explore various supportive therapies for depression, providing valuable insights into a holistic approach to healing mental health disorders.

1. Mindfulness Meditation: Mindfulness meditation involves focusing one's attention on the present moment, without judgment. This practice helps individuals develop a greater sense of self-awareness and acceptance, leading to reduced stress levels and improved emotional well-being. Regular mindfulness meditation has been shown to alleviate depressive symptoms and cultivate a positive mindset.

2. Exercise and Physical Activity: Engaging in regular exercise and physical activity has been proven to have a positive impact on mental health, including depression. Physical activity stimulates the release of endorphins, also known as "feel-good" hormones, which can elevate mood and reduce symptoms of depression. Incorporating activities such as walking, jogging, yoga, or dancing into your routine can make a significant difference in managing depressive symptoms.

3. Nutrition and Diet: A well-balanced diet plays a crucial role in supporting mental health. Certain nutrients, such as omega-3 fatty acids found in fish, nuts, and seeds, have been linked to a lower risk of depression. Additionally, avoiding processed foods, excessive sugar, and caffeine can help stabilize mood and energy levels. Including a variety of fresh fruits, vegetables, whole grains, and lean proteins in your diet can contribute to overall well-being.

4. Social Support: Building a strong support network is vital for individuals with depression. Surrounding yourself with positive and understanding individuals can provide emotional support,

encouragement, and a sense of belonging. Participating in support groups or seeking therapy can also offer a safe space to share experiences and gain insights from others facing similar challenges.

5. Alternative Therapies: Several alternative therapies, such as acupuncture, aromatherapy, and herbal supplements, have shown promising results in managing depression. While these therapies may not be suitable for everyone, some individuals find them beneficial in reducing depressive symptoms and promoting relaxation and overall well-being.

It is important to note that while these supportive therapies can be highly effective, they should not replace professional medical advice or prescribed treatments. It is recommended to consult with a healthcare professional before incorporating any new therapies into your depression management plan.

By adopting a holistic approach that combines medication, psychotherapy, and supportive therapies, individuals can unlock happiness and work towards healing their mental health disorders. Understanding that depression can be managed through various avenues empowers individuals to take an active role in their mental well-being and pursue a healthier, happier lifestyle.

Chapter 5: Managing Anxiety Disorders

Recognizing Anxiety Disorders: Types and Symptoms

Anxiety disorders have become increasingly prevalent in our modern society, affecting individuals of all ages and backgrounds. In this subchapter, we will delve into the various types of anxiety disorders and their associated symptoms. By understanding these conditions, anyone can gain a deeper insight into their own mental health or that of their loved ones, paving the way for a proactive approach to healing and happiness.

Generalized Anxiety Disorder (GAD) is one of the most common anxiety disorders, characterized by excessive worry and fear about everyday life events. People with GAD often experience restlessness, irritability, difficulty concentrating, and physical symptoms such as muscle tension and sleep disturbances.

Panic Disorder is another type of anxiety disorder that manifests in recurring panic attacks. These attacks are intense and sudden, accompanied by symptoms such as a racing heart, shortness of breath, dizziness, and a sense of impending doom. Panic attacks can be incredibly distressing and may lead individuals to avoid certain places or situations for fear of triggering another attack.

Social Anxiety Disorder (SAD) is characterized by an intense fear of social situations and the fear of being judged or humiliated by others. People with SAD often experience extreme self-consciousness, blushing, trembling, and have a tendency to avoid social interactions altogether.

Post-Traumatic Stress Disorder (PTSD) is an anxiety disorder that develops after experiencing or witnessing a traumatic event. Individuals with PTSD may relive the traumatic event through nightmares or flashbacks, experience severe anxiety, have difficulty sleeping, and become emotionally detached.

Obsessive-Compulsive Disorder (OCD) is characterized by intrusive thoughts (obsessions) and repetitive behaviors (compulsions) that individuals feel compelled to perform. These obsessions and compulsions can significantly interfere with daily life, causing distress and anxiety.

Phobias are intense and irrational fears of specific objects, situations, or activities. Common phobias include a fear of heights (acrophobia), spiders (arachnophobia), and flying (aviophobia). Individuals with phobias often go to great lengths to avoid triggering their fears.

Recognizing the symptoms associated with these anxiety disorders is crucial for early intervention and effective treatment. By understanding the various types of anxiety disorders and their manifestations, readers can gain valuable knowledge to help themselves or others who may be struggling. Remember, seeking professional help from mental health experts is always advisable when dealing with anxiety disorders, as they can provide the necessary guidance and support to unlock happiness and heal from within.

In the upcoming chapters, we will explore holistic approaches to managing anxiety disorders, including lifestyle changes, therapy techniques, and self-care practices that can support overall mental well-being.

Conventional Treatments for Anxiety Disorders

Anxiety disorders can be debilitating and have a significant impact on one's daily life. Fortunately, there are several conventional treatments available that can help individuals manage and overcome their anxiety. In this subchapter, we will explore some of the most commonly used conventional treatments for anxiety disorders.

1. Medication: One of the most prevalent forms of treatment for anxiety disorders is medication. Antidepressants, selective serotonin reuptake inhibitors (SSRIs), and benzodiazepines are commonly prescribed to help alleviate symptoms of anxiety. These medications work by balancing the chemicals in the brain responsible for regulating mood and emotions.

2. Cognitive-Behavioral Therapy (CBT): CBT is a widely recognized and effective treatment for anxiety disorders. This therapy focuses on identifying and challenging negative thought patterns and replacing them with more positive and realistic ones. Through CBT, individuals learn coping strategies and develop skills to manage their anxiety effectively.

3. Exposure Therapy: Exposure therapy is often used for specific phobias and panic disorders. It involves gradually exposing individuals to their fears in a controlled and safe environment. Over time, this exposure helps individuals confront and overcome their anxieties, leading to a reduction in symptoms.

4. Relaxation Techniques: Various relaxation techniques, such as deep breathing exercises, progressive muscle relaxation, and meditation, can help individuals manage their anxiety symptoms. These techniques promote a sense of calmness and relaxation, reducing the body's stress response.

5. Support Groups: Joining support groups can be immensely beneficial for individuals with anxiety disorders. Sharing experiences, concerns, and strategies with others facing similar challenges can provide a sense of belonging and understanding. Support groups also offer an opportunity to learn from others who have successfully managed their anxiety.

6. Lifestyle Changes: Making certain lifestyle changes can significantly impact anxiety levels. Regular exercise, maintaining a healthy diet, getting enough sleep, and reducing caffeine and alcohol intake can all contribute to improved mental well-being.

It is essential to remember that each individual's experience with anxiety disorders is unique, and what works for one person may not work for another. Therefore, it is crucial to consult with a healthcare professional to determine the most suitable treatment plan.

In conclusion, conventional treatments for anxiety disorders encompass a range of approaches, including medication, therapy, relaxation techniques, support groups, and lifestyle changes. By exploring and utilizing these treatment options, individuals with anxiety disorders can find relief and take steps towards unlocking happiness and healing their mental health.

Holistic Approaches to Coping with Anxiety

Anxiety has become a prevalent concern in our fast-paced, modern society. It affects people of all ages and backgrounds, contributing to the rise of lifestyle diseases. While medication and therapy are commonly prescribed methods for managing anxiety, there is a growing interest in holistic approaches that address the root causes of this mental health disorder. In this subchapter, we explore various holistic techniques and lifestyle changes that can help individuals cope with anxiety and promote overall well-being.

One fundamental aspect of holistic healing is the recognition that the mind and body are interconnected. By nourishing both aspects, one can alleviate anxiety symptoms and enhance mental and physical well-being. One effective technique is mindfulness meditation, which involves focusing attention on the present moment without judgment. Research has shown that regular meditation practice can reduce anxiety levels, calm the mind, and promote a sense of inner peace.

Another holistic approach to managing anxiety is through proper nutrition. It is not surprising that what we eat can affect our mental health. Consuming a balanced diet rich in fruits, vegetables, whole grains, and lean proteins can provide essential nutrients that support brain health and stabilize mood. Additionally, certain foods like chamomile tea, dark chocolate, and omega-3 fatty acids found in fish have been shown to have calming effects on the nervous system.

Physical activity is also an integral part of a holistic approach to coping with anxiety. Engaging in regular exercise not only improves cardiovascular health but also releases endorphins, the body's natural mood boosters. Whether it's going for a walk, practicing yoga, or participating in a team sport, finding an enjoyable physical activity can significantly reduce anxiety levels and enhance overall well-being.

Holistic approaches to anxiety also emphasize the importance of self-care practices. This includes getting enough sleep, setting boundaries, practicing self-compassion, and engaging in activities that bring joy and relaxation. Taking time for oneself allows for rejuvenation and stress reduction, ultimately helping to manage anxiety.

In conclusion, holistic approaches to coping with anxiety offer a comprehensive and interconnected way to address the root causes of this mental health disorder. By incorporating techniques such as mindfulness meditation, proper nutrition, regular physical activity, and self-care practices, individuals can experience a significant reduction in anxiety symptoms and improve their overall well-being. It is important to remember that everyone's journey to healing is unique, so finding the right combination of holistic approaches that work for you is essential. By adopting these holistic techniques, individuals can unlock happiness and take control of their mental health.

Relaxation Techniques for Anxiety Relief

In today's fast-paced world, anxiety has become a common companion for many individuals. The constant pressure to meet deadlines, maintain relationships, and juggle multiple responsibilities can take a toll on our mental health. However, there are numerous relaxation techniques that can help alleviate anxiety and promote a sense of calm and well-being. In this subchapter, we will explore some effective strategies to find anxiety relief and unlock happiness.

One powerful technique is deep breathing. When we are anxious, our breathing tends to become shallow and rapid, exacerbating our stress levels. By consciously practicing deep breathing, we can activate our body's relaxation response. Find a quiet space, sit comfortably, and take a slow, deep breath in through your nose, allowing your belly to expand. Hold it for a few seconds, and then exhale slowly through your mouth. Repeat this process several times, focusing on the sensation of your breath entering and leaving your body. Deep breathing can help calm the nervous system and reduce anxiety levels.

Another effective relaxation technique is progressive muscle relaxation. This method involves tensing and then releasing each muscle group in the body, promoting a deep sense of relaxation. Start by tensing the muscles in your feet, and then gradually work your way up, including your legs, abdomen, arms, and face. Hold the tension for a few seconds, and then release, allowing the muscles to relax completely. This exercise helps to release physical tension and can be particularly beneficial for individuals who experience muscle tightness due to anxiety.

Meditation and mindfulness practices are also highly recommended for anxiety relief. By focusing on the present moment and observing our thoughts without judgment, we can detach from anxious thinking patterns. Find a quiet space, sit in a comfortable position, and close your eyes. Bring your attention to your breath, allowing your thoughts to come and go without attachment. With regular practice, meditation can help rewire our brains and reduce anxiety symptoms.

Incorporating regular exercise into our routine is another essential aspect of anxiety relief. Exercise releases endorphins, which are natural mood-boosting chemicals in the brain. Engaging in activities such as walking, jogging, yoga, or dancing can help reduce anxiety and promote a sense of overall well-being.

In conclusion, anxiety can be a challenging hurdle to overcome, but with the right relaxation techniques, we can find relief and unlock happiness. Whether it's through deep breathing, progressive muscle relaxation, meditation, or exercise, incorporating these practices into our daily lives can help manage anxiety and promote a healthier, more balanced lifestyle. Remember, taking care of our mental health is just as important as tending to our physical well-being, and by prioritizing relaxation, we can unlock a happier and more fulfilling life.

Herbal Remedies for Anxiety

In today's fast-paced and demanding world, anxiety has become an all-too-common condition affecting people of all ages and backgrounds. While conventional treatments such as therapy and medication are often effective, many individuals are seeking natural alternatives to manage their anxiety. This subchapter explores the potential benefits of herbal remedies for anxiety, providing readers with a holistic approach to healing mental health disorders.

1. Chamomile: Chamomile has long been recognized for its calming properties. This herb can be consumed as a tea, helping to relax the mind and reduce anxiety symptoms. Its soothing effects can promote better sleep, making it an excellent choice for those struggling with insomnia caused by anxiety.

2. Lavender: Lavender is known for its pleasant aroma and calming effects. Whether used in essential oil form or added to bathwater, lavender can help alleviate anxiety symptoms and promote relaxation. Its aromatic properties have been shown to reduce stress levels and ease tension in the body.

3. Valerian Root: Valerian root is a potent herb that has been used for centuries to treat anxiety and insomnia. This herb can be consumed as a supplement or tea, helping to calm the nervous system and promote a sense of tranquility. Valerian root is particularly beneficial for individuals experiencing anxiety-related sleep disturbances.

4. Lemon Balm: Lemon balm is a versatile herb that offers various health benefits, including anxiety relief. Consuming lemon balm tea or supplements can help reduce nervousness and promote a sense of calm. This herb also aids in improving sleep quality and reducing restlessness.

5. Passionflower: Passionflower is a powerful herbal remedy that has been used for centuries to alleviate anxiety symptoms. Its calming properties can help reduce anxiety-induced racing thoughts and promote relaxation. Passionflower is often consumed as a tea or supplement.

While herbal remedies can be helpful in managing anxiety, it is essential to consult with a healthcare professional before incorporating them into your treatment plan. They can provide guidance on appropriate dosages and potential interactions with any existing medications.

Remember, anxiety is a complex condition, and self-care practices such as exercise, meditation, and maintaining a healthy lifestyle are equally important in managing symptoms. By adopting a holistic approach and incorporating herbal remedies into your routine, you can unlock happiness and take control of your mental health.

Mind-Body Practices for Anxiety Management

In our fast-paced, modern world, anxiety has become an all-too-common companion for many people. Whether it's triggered by work pressures, financial strain, or personal relationships, anxiety can take a toll on our mental and physical well-being. However, there is hope. In this subchapter, we explore mind-body practices as powerful tools for managing anxiety and finding inner peace.

1. Meditation: Meditation is a practice that involves training the mind to focus and redirect thoughts. By regularly setting aside time to meditate, individuals can cultivate a sense of calm and clarity. Research has shown that meditation can significantly reduce anxiety symptoms and improve overall mental health. Whether you choose to practice mindfulness meditation, loving-kindness meditation, or transcendental meditation, the benefits are profound.

2. Yoga: Yoga combines physical postures, breathing exercises, and meditation to promote relaxation and reduce stress. The gentle movements and deep breathing in yoga help activate the body's relaxation response, counteracting the fight-or-flight response associated with anxiety. Regular yoga practice can increase self-awareness, reduce muscle tension, and improve sleep, all of which contribute to anxiety management.

3. Tai Chi: Originating in ancient China, Tai Chi is a gentle form of exercise that involves slow, flowing movements and deep breathing. This mind-body practice has been shown to reduce anxiety and improve overall well-being. Tai Chi promotes relaxation, improves balance, and enhances physical coordination. By focusing on the present moment and coordinating movement with breath, individuals can experience a sense of calm and inner peace.

4. Breathing Techniques: Deep breathing exercises can be incredibly effective in reducing anxiety symptoms. By consciously slowing down and deepening the breath, you activate the body's relaxation response. Techniques such as

diaphragmatic breathing, box breathing, and alternate nostril breathing can help regulate the nervous system and reduce anxiety levels.

5. Progressive Muscle Relaxation: This technique involves tensing and then releasing different muscle groups, promoting physical relaxation and reducing tension. By systematically relaxing each muscle group, individuals can release physical tension that often accompanies anxiety. Regular practice of progressive muscle relaxation can improve overall well-being and provide a sense of control over anxiety symptoms.

Incorporating mind-body practices into your daily routine can be a powerful way to manage anxiety and promote overall mental health. By tapping into the mind-body connection, you can find inner peace and unlock happiness. Experiment with these practices, find what resonates with you, and commit to a regular practice. With time and dedication, you can experience the transformative power of mind-body practices and discover a life free from the grips of anxiety.

Chapter 6: Nurturing Mental Well-being

Building Resilience and Emotional Intelligence

In today's fast-paced and stressful world, it is crucial to develop resilience and emotional intelligence to effectively deal with the challenges of life. In this subchapter, we will explore how building these essential skills can help anyone, especially those affected by lifestyle diseases, to unlock happiness and heal mental health disorders.

Resilience is the ability to bounce back from setbacks and adapt to difficult situations. It is not about avoiding stress or living a life free from problems, but rather about developing the strength and flexibility to cope with them. People with resilience have a positive mindset, strong problem-solving skills, and the ability to manage their emotions effectively.

One of the key components of building resilience is self-awareness. Understanding our own emotions, strengths, and limitations allows us to navigate through life with greater ease. By recognizing our triggers and developing healthy coping mechanisms, we can prevent stress from overwhelming us and negatively impacting our mental health.

Another crucial aspect is building a support system. Surrounding ourselves with positive and empathetic individuals who can offer guidance and support during challenging times can significantly enhance our resilience. Additionally, seeking professional help, such as therapy or counseling, can provide valuable tools and strategies to manage stress and build resilience.

Emotional intelligence, on the other hand, refers to our ability to understand and manage our own emotions and effectively communicate and empathize with others. By honing this skill, we can improve our relationships, make better decisions, and handle conflicts more effectively, all of which contribute to overall mental well-being.

Practicing mindfulness and self-care are essential in developing emotional intelligence. Taking time to reflect on our emotions, thoughts, and behaviors can help us better understand ourselves and others. Engaging in activities that bring us joy and relaxation, such as exercise, meditation, or pursuing hobbies, can also help reduce stress and enhance emotional well-being.

In conclusion, building resilience and emotional intelligence is vital for anyone, particularly those affected by lifestyle diseases, to unlock happiness and heal mental health disorders. By developing these skills, we can effectively manage stress, adapt to challenges, and cultivate healthier relationships. Remember, it is never too late to start building resilience and emotional intelligence – small steps taken today can lead to significant positive changes in the future.

Enhancing Self-Esteem and Self-Compassion

In today's fast-paced and demanding world, it is no surprise that many people struggle with low self-esteem and self-compassion. These issues can greatly impact our mental health and contribute to the development of lifestyle diseases. However, there are steps we can take to enhance our self-esteem and cultivate self-compassion, leading to a healthier and happier life.

Self-esteem is how we perceive ourselves and our worth. It plays a significant role in our overall well-being and affects our relationships, career, and personal growth. To enhance self-esteem, it is crucial to start by recognizing and challenging negative self-talk. Often, we are our harshest critics, and this negative self-talk can be detrimental to our self-esteem. By consciously replacing negative thoughts with positive affirmations and practicing self-compassion, we can begin to change our perception of ourselves.

Self-compassion is the practice of treating ourselves with kindness and understanding, especially during times of struggle or failure. It involves acknowledging our flaws and mistakes without judgment or self-criticism. Cultivating self-compassion allows us to develop resilience and bounce back from setbacks, fostering a sense of worthiness and acceptance.

One effective way to enhance self-esteem and self-compassion is through self-care. Taking care of our physical, emotional, and mental well-being is essential for building a positive self-image. Engaging in activities that bring us joy, practicing mindfulness and relaxation techniques, and maintaining a healthy lifestyle can significantly impact our self-esteem and overall happiness.

Another powerful tool for enhancing self-esteem and self-compassion is surrounding ourselves with supportive and positive individuals. Building a strong network of friends, family, or even joining support groups can provide a safe space for validation, understanding, and encouragement. Sharing our struggles and achievements with others who genuinely care helps us feel valued and reinforces our self-worth.

Furthermore, setting realistic goals and celebrating small victories along the way can boost self-esteem. It is important to remember that self-esteem is not solely based on external achievements but rather on how we perceive ourselves. By acknowledging and appreciating our accomplishments, no matter how small, we can reinforce a positive self-image and cultivate self-compassion.

In conclusion, enhancing self-esteem and self-compassion is crucial for maintaining mental health and preventing lifestyle diseases. By challenging negative self-talk, practicing self-care, surrounding ourselves with supportive individuals, and celebrating our achievements, we can build a healthier and happier life. Remember, self-esteem is not a destination but a journey, and with consistent effort and self-compassion, we can unlock true happiness and healing.

Cultivating Positive Habits and Mindsets

Developing and maintaining healthy and advantageous ways of thinking and doing is the process of cultivating positive habits and attitudes. It entails making deliberate decisions regarding our actions, thoughts, and interactions with the outside environment.

It is possible to develop positive habits and mindsets in a variety of ways. Here are few instances:

Embrace thankfulness. You can refocus your attention to the positive by taking the time to acknowledge and be grateful for all of life's blessings, no matter how minor. Consider maintaining a thankfulness diary, or just spend a few minutes every day thinking about what you have to be thankful for.

Dispute pessimistic thoughts. Consider whether a negative notion is truly true whenever you have one. Is there proof in favor of it? Or is it just a mental habit? Try to replace it with a more realistic and upbeat notion if it's not true.

Make constructive goals. Setting and achieving objectives can help you feel motivated and purposeful. Ensure that your objectives are in line with your priorities and values, and that they are both attainable and practical.

Spend time with upbeat individuals. Your perspective and emotional state can be greatly influenced by the individuals you spend time with. Be in the company of positive, upbeat, and supporting individuals who lift your spirits.

Look for your own needs. This include maintaining a nutritious diet, getting enough rest, and engaging in regular exercise. Maintaining your physical well-being might benefit your mental well-being as well.

It takes time and work to develop great habits and mindsets, but the effort is worthwhile. Happiness, achievement, and general well-being are more likely to come to those with an optimistic attitude.

Here are some more pointers for developing uplifting routines and attitudes:

Begin modestly. Avoid attempting to make all the changes at once. Choose one or two areas that you would like to improve, and concentrate on those.

Have patience. Creating new habits and altering your thinking takes time. If you don't notice results right away, don't give up. You'll ultimately notice a difference if you just keep practicing.

Take care of yourself. Everyone makes mistakes occasionally. It's important to not punish yourself for mistakes you make. Simply own your error and move on.

Honor your accomplishments. Spend some time celebrating your accomplishments when you reach your goals. This will support your motivation and forward motion.

Developing constructive routines and attitudes takes time. You can continue to work on it throughout your life. However, it's an investment that pays off handsomely.

Harnessing the Power of Social Support

The network of people that support us financially, practically, and emotionally is known as social support. It can involve our friends, neighbors, coworkers, family, and other community members.

While social support is crucial for everyone, those who are dealing with mental health issues especially need it. Social support has been shown to lower stress, elevate mood, and increase self-worth. It can also provide them a feeling of purpose and community.

Utilizing the benefits of social support for mental health can take numerous forms. Here are few instances:

Speak to a reliable person. Speak with a friend, relative, therapist, or other someone you can trust when you're feeling down and need assistance.

Sign up for a support group. Joining a support group is a fantastic opportunity to meet others who are experiencing similar things. They can offer you a sense of belonging, as well as helpful guidance and emotional support.

Participate in your local community. Building relationships and meeting new people might be facilitated by volunteering or taking part in other community activities. It can also make you feel fulfilled and like you have a purpose.

The following are some further pointers for maximizing the benefits of social support for mental health:

Talk freely about your difficulties. It's critical to be honest about your mental health struggles with friends and family. This will enable them to better comprehend your situation and get you the assistance you require.

Establish limits. Establishing limits with your social support system is crucial. Inform them of your needs for support and your capacity for it.

Never hesitate to seek for assistance. Never be embarrassed to ask for assistance if you need it. Your family and friends are there to help you.

One of the most effective tools for managing mental health issues is social support. You may raise your general well-being, lessen stress, and elevate your mood by utilizing the power of social support.

Embracing Spirituality and Purpose

Accepting spirituality and purpose entails discovering a purpose and significance in life that extends beyond this planet. It may entail making a connection with a spiritual community, a higher power, or just a strong sense of meaning and purpose.

Spirituality and purpose can be embraced in a multitude of ways. While some people discover spirituality via religion, others discover it via other disciplines, nature, or meditation. In the end, each person must determine what is most effective for them.

Developing a sense of purpose and spirituality can be very beneficial to mental health. It can support:

Decrease worry and tension

Enhance resilience and coping mechanisms; raise self-worth and confidence; elevate mood and emotional well-being;

Give life a feeling of direction and significance.

A number of actions can be taken if you are interested in embracing spirituality and purpose:

Investigate various spiritual practices. Choose a spiritual tradition that speaks to you by taking your time and exploring the many options available.

Make contact with a religious community. There are numerous options available if you're interested in joining a religious community. See if any of your friends and family have any recommendations, or look up local religious communities online.

Think. Finding inner peace and tranquillity and establishing a connection with yourself can be achieved via meditation. Choose a meditation style that suits you best from the numerous available options, then stick with it.

Embrace thankfulness. You can focus on the positive and cultivate a more spiritual perspective by taking the time to enjoy the good things in your life. Consider maintaining a thankfulness diary, or just spend a few minutes every day thinking about what you have to be thankful for.

Discover your mission. What provides purpose to your life? What inspires you greatly? Find your life's meaning by giving these questions some thought. You can begin living your life in accordance with your mission once you are aware of it.

Accepting spirituality and meaning in life is a process rather than a final goal. Developing a spiritual practice and discovering your life's purpose requires time and work. However, the journey is definitely worthwhile.

Here are some more pointers for embracing your purpose and spirituality:

Have an open mind. There's no one correct approach to discover your purpose in life or to be spiritual. Keep an open mind as you investigate many options to see which one suits you the best.

Have patience. Establishing a spiritual practice and discovering your life's purpose takes time. If you don't notice results right away, don't give up. If you simply keep trying and exploring, you will ultimately figure things out.

Take care of yourself. All people make mistakes when they are growing spiritually. Don't berate yourself if you make a mistake. Simply own your error and move on.

Locate a mentor or advisor. Asking someone who is spiritually mature in your life to be your mentor or guide might be a good idea. As you travel on your spiritual path, they can provide you insight, support, and guidance.

Accepting spirituality and purpose in one's life can have profound effects. It can support you in leading a more purposeful and happy life.

Chapter 7: Maintaining Long-Term Mental Health

Preventing Relapse and Recurrence

Relapse is the recurrence of symptoms following a period of abstinence. A mental health disorder's recurrence is a fresh episode that occurs following a time of remission.

You may take a lot of steps to stop a mental health issue from relapsing or returning. Here are a few pointers:

Maintain your drug regimen. Even if you are feeling better, it is crucial that you take your medicine as directed if you have been prescribed it for a mental health condition. Your chance of relapsing can rise if you stop taking your prescription.

Keep up your therapy. Therapy can assist you in recognizing and controlling your triggers, creating coping skills, and assembling a network of support. Even after you start to feel better, you should still attend treatment sessions in order to help yourself avoid relapsing.

Look for your own needs. This include maintaining a nutritious diet, obtaining enough rest, working out frequently, and abstaining from drugs and alcohol. Maintaining your physical well-being can enhance your mental well-being and vice versa.

Determine what triggers you. You can create management plans for your triggers once you are aware of them. For instance, you can attempt to avoid specific people or develop coping mechanisms for their company if you are aware that they frequently cause you worry.

Create constructive coping strategies. Coping mechanisms are strategies for handling stress and challenging feelings. You may control your emotions in a positive and healthy way by using healthy coping strategies. Here are a few instances of constructive coping techniques:

Work out

methods of relaxation (such as yoga, meditation, and deep breathing)

Having time with those you love

Taking part in interests and pastimes you find enjoyable

Getting expert assistance

Create a solid support system. Everyone benefits from having a solid support system, but those who struggle with mental health issues most of all. You can get practical guidance, emotional support, and a feeling of community from your support system. Family, friends, therapists, support groups, and other individuals who are aware of your situation can all be a part of your support system.

Seek expert assistance as required. Never be reluctant to seek professional assistance if you are finding it difficult to manage your mental health on your own. A therapist can offer you support, assist in creating a treatment plan, and teach you coping mechanisms.

It is crucial to keep in mind that relapses and recurrences are typical. It does not indicate failure if you do experience a relapse or recurrence. It simply implies that you need to modify your treatment plan and create new coping mechanisms in collaboration with your therapist.

Here are some more pointers to avoid relapses and recurrences:

Tell the truth to yourself. Tell your therapist and yourself the truth if you believe you are headed for a relapse. Getting assistance early on is preferable to waiting until things worsen.

Never hesitate to seek for assistance. Don't be scared to seek your therapist, family, friends, or other support system members for assistance if you need it managing your mental health.

Have patience. Recuperation is a lengthy process. If you don't notice results right away, don't give up. If you persevere, you will eventually accomplish your objectives.

It is possible to stop a mental health problem from relapsing or returning. You can lessen the likelihood of relapsing and lead a long, healthy life by heeding the advice provided above.

Strategies for Stress Management

There are numerous approaches of managing stress. Here are few instances:

Get moving. One excellent method to lower stress and elevate mood is to exercise. On most days of the week, try to get in at least 30 minutes of moderate-intensity exercise.

methods for relaxation. Stress and anxiety can be lessened by practicing relaxation techniques like yoga, meditation, and deep breathing. There are a plethora of relaxation techniques at your disposal; pick one that suits you well and stay with it.

management of time. You can feel more in control of your life and experience less stress by developing good time management skills. Establish reasonable timelines and goals, and divide difficult jobs into smaller, more doable ones.

social assistance. You can feel less alone and more supported by talking about your issues and spending time with loved ones. If you don't have a solid support system in place for yourself, you might want to join a support group for those dealing with stress or other mental health issues.

Take care of yourself. Taking care of oneself is crucial to stress management and mental wellness preservation. Make sure you consume a balanced diet, get adequate sleep, and abstain from drugs and alcohol.

Here are a few more stress-reduction suggestions:

Decide what stresses you out. Which items are causing you stress? Once you are aware of your stressors, you can begin to create coping mechanisms.

Take pauses. Take a few minutes to relax and remove yourself from the situation if you're feeling overwhelmed. Take a stroll, enjoy some music, or practice deep breathing.

No, say. Saying no to requests is acceptable, particularly if you're feeling overburdened. It's okay to establish limits and guard your time.

Seek out expert assistance. Speak with a therapist or counselor if you're finding it difficult to control your stress on your own. They can assist you in creating a stress management strategy and teach you coping mechanisms.

Although stress is a natural part of life, it's crucial to have appropriate coping mechanisms. You can lower your stress levels and enhance your general well-being by heeding the advice provided above.

Continuing Self-Care Practices

Continuing self-care practices is important for maintaining good mental health and well-being. Self-care is the practice of taking care of yourself physically, emotionally, and mentally. It can involve doing things that you enjoy, that make you feel good, and that help you to manage stress.

There are many different self-care practices that you can do on a regular basis. Here are a few examples:

- Spend time in nature. Spending time in nature has been shown to have a number of benefits for mental health, including reducing stress, improving mood, and boosting creativity. Go for a walk in the park, sit by a river, or hike through the woods.

- Meditate. Meditation is a practice that involves focusing your attention on the present moment. It can help to reduce stress, anxiety, and depression. There are many different types of meditation, so find one that works for you and stick with it.

- Read a book. Reading can be a great way to relax and escape from the stresses of everyday life. It can also help to improve your vocabulary and imagination. Choose a book that you're interested in and enjoy the read.

- Spend time with loved ones. Spending time with loved ones can help you to feel connected and supported. It can also help to reduce stress and improve your mood. Make time for the people who matter most to you.

- Get enough sleep. Sleep is essential for good mental and physical health. Aim for 7-8 hours of sleep per night.

- Eat a healthy diet. Eating a healthy diet can help you to feel better physically and mentally. Make sure to eat plenty of fruits, vegetables, and whole grains. Avoid processed foods, sugary drinks, and excessive amounts of caffeine and alcohol.

- Exercise regularly. Exercise is a great way to reduce stress, improve mood, and boost energy levels. Aim for at least 30 minutes of moderate-intensity exercise most days of the week.

- Do something creative. Engaging in creative activities can help to reduce stress, improve mood, and boost self-esteem. Try painting, drawing, writing, playing music, or gardening.

- Take a break from social media. Social media can be a great way to stay connected with friends and family, but it can also be a source of stress and anxiety. Take a break from social media for a few days or weeks and see how you feel.

It is important to find self-care practices that work for you and that you enjoy. Make time for self-care on a regular basis, even if it's just for a few minutes each day. Continuing self-care practices can help you to maintain good mental health and well-being.

Here are some additional tips for continuing self-care practices:

- Make self-care a priority. Schedule self-care activities into your calendar and treat them as important appointments.

- Be flexible. If you don't have time for your usual self-care routine, find a shorter or modified version that you can do.

- Be kind to yourself. Don't beat yourself up if you miss a self-care activity. Just pick up where you left off and keep going.

- Celebrate your successes. When you stick to your self-care routine, take the time to celebrate your successes. This will help you to stay motivated and keep going.

Continuing self-care practices is essential for maintaining good mental health and well-being. By following the tips above, you can make self-care a part of your daily routine and reap the many benefits.

Advocacy and Support for Mental Health Awareness

In order to decrease stigma, increase access to care, and increase public knowledge of mental health issues, mental health advocacy and support are crucial. There are numerous approaches to promoting and supporting mental health awareness. Here are few instances:

Tell your tale. Telling your own story is one of the most effective methods to promote mental health awareness. This can assist in dispelling stigma and letting others know they're not alone. You can talk at public gatherings, make a blog entry, or share your experience on social media.

Teach others and yourself. There will be less stigma associated with mental health issues the more people are aware of them. Find out about various mental health issues, including what causes them, how they manifest, and available treatments. Talk to people about what you've learned, particularly your friends, family, and coworkers.

Participate in your local community. You can become involved with a variety of mental health advocacy organizations and support groups. To support their efforts, you can attend events, give money, or offer your time as a volunteer.

Make contact with the people you elected. Inform your political representatives of your support for initiatives that increase access to care and how important mental health is to you. Your elected representatives can be contacted via phone, email, or letter.

Additional advice for promoting and encouraging mental health awareness is provided below:

Show reverence. Respect those who have mental health conditions and their experiences while having conversations about mental health. Steer clear of stigmatizing language.

Be encouraging. Be encouraging and willing to assist someone you know who is experiencing mental health issues. Show them that you care about them and that you are available to them.

Have patience. Adjustment takes time. If you don't notice results right away, don't give up. Eventually, if we continue to promote and advocate for mental health awareness, things will start to change.

In order to create a society where everyone feels comfortable discussing their mental health and obtaining the necessary care, mental health advocacy and support are crucial. You may improve the lives of those with mental health issues and their families by heeding the advice provided here.

The Importance of Regular Check-ups and Monitoring

It's critical to have regular monitoring and examinations for mental wellness. You ought to visit a mental health specialist on a regular basis, much like you would for a medical examination.

Your mental health expert will inquire about your behavior, thoughts, feelings, and mood during a mental health check-up. They will also evaluate your general mental health and well-being as well as your risk factors for mental health issues.

Frequent mental health examinations can aid in the early detection of possible mental health issues, when they are most amenable to treatment. Your long-term prognosis may be improved and mental health issues may be kept from getting worse with early detection and treatment.

Regular check-ups not only help spot any mental health issues early on, but they can also assist you in:

Check the efficacy of your treatment regimen.

As necessary, modify your treatment strategy.

Discover fresh coping mechanisms and stress-reduction techniques.

Establish a cordial rapport with your mental health specialist.

Develop your mental health and resilience.

It is especially crucial to get frequent check-ups and monitoring if you are dealing with mental health issues. You can stay on track with your treatment plan and manage your symptoms with the support of your mental health expert.

Here are some more pointers regarding the significance of routine evaluations and observations for mental health:

Be truthful with both your mental health provider and yourself. It's critical to be open and truthful about your feelings and life events with both your mental health provider and yourself. This will enable them to give you the finest treatment possible.

Never hesitate to seek for assistance. Never hesitate to seek assistance from a mental health professional if you need it. They are there to encourage and assist you in recovering.

Have patience. It takes time to heal. If you don't notice results right away, don't give up. You will eventually achieve your goals if you just keep working with your mental health practitioner.

Having regular evaluations and supervision is crucial to preserving mental wellness. You may enhance your general well-being and get the most out of your mental health treatment by heeding the advice provided above.

Conclusion: Embracing a Holistic Journey to Happiness and Mental Health

Taking care of your physical, mental, emotional, and spiritual needs is a crucial part of embracing a holistic approach to happiness and mental wellness. It entails leading a life that is consistent with your values and objectives and making decisions that promote your general well-being.

Embracing a holistic approach to happiness and mental health can take many forms. Here are some pointers:

Ensure your bodily well-being. This include maintaining a nutritious diet, exercising frequently, and obtaining adequate rest. You feel better both physically and psychologically when you take good care of your physical health.

Engage in meditation and mindfulness. The practice of mindfulness involves focusing attention on the current moment without passing judgment. Concentrating your concentration on a single thing or idea is the practice of meditation. Numerous advantages of mindfulness and meditation for mental health have been demonstrated, including a decrease in stress, anxiety, and sadness.

Establish connections. Having social support is essential for mental wellness. Participate in voluntary work in your neighborhood, join a club, or spend time with loved ones. You can feel more a part of the world and supported when you interact with other people.

Return favors to others. One of the best ways to improve your own happiness and sense of wellbeing is to help others. Give of your time to a cause that matters to you or just be kind to others.

Have a life with a purpose. Possessing a purpose in life might help you feel meaningful and directed. Which values do you hold? What are the objectives? What goals do you have for your life? Discover what makes your life meaningful, then live it to the fullest.

It takes a lifetime to embrace a holistic path to happiness and mental wellness. It's not something you can accomplish quickly. But you may start to go in the correct way by implementing little adjustments in your day-to-day activities.

Here are some more pointers for welcoming a comprehensive path to mental wellness and happiness:

Give yourself some time and kindness. Adjustment takes time. If you don't notice results right away, don't give up. If you persevere, you will eventually accomplish your objectives.

Honor your accomplishments. As you advance, remember to acknowledge and appreciate your accomplishments. This will support your motivation and perseverance.

Seek expert assistance as required. Never be reluctant to seek professional assistance if you are finding it difficult to manage your mental health on your own. A therapist can offer you support, assist in creating a treatment plan, and teach you coping mechanisms.

Taking a comprehensive approach to achieving happiness and mental well-being is among the best things you can do for yourself. It's definitely an investment that pays off.